This newest book by Bishop Harry Jackson is powerful! It is clear, compelling, convincing, and convicting. Read it and be blessed! Then buy copies for your friends.

—*Rick Warren*
Pastor, Saddleback Church
Best-Selling Author, *The Purpose-Driven Life*

The image of America today is no longer one of a tall Uncle Sam in a big patriotic hat, waving and smiling at the crowd during a Fourth of July parade. People are angry—and rightly so. But rioting and looting is *not* the answer. The good news is the answer can be found right here in this book. *A Manifesto: Christian America's Contract with Minorities* by my good friend, Bishop Harry R. Jackson Jr., lays out a course for all races and creeds to come together and work for a better tomorrow for everyone.

—*Robert Morris*
Founding Lead Senior Pastor, Gateway Church
Best-Selling Author, *The Blessed Life, Beyond Blessed* and *Take the Day Off*

Bishop Harry Jackson has been at the forefront of healing the racial divide in America. Several years ago, he asked me to help encourage reconciliation in the church and nation. It has been my honor to work alongside him. He has built on this platform with the release of a Christ-centered manifesto, using the acronym "EMPOWERED" to provide a biblical agenda for social correction in America. By weaving in personal stories he has experienced as a black man, his suggested guidelines for reform come alive. I consider Bishop Harry Jackson to be one of the greatest, most courageous, and compassionate leaders I've ever known. He truly loves his neighbor and with all his heart wants God's best for everyone on this planet. He will prove to be a major factor in preserving our precious freedom and healing racial misunderstanding and hurt. Please read this great book, as you will hear not only the bishop's heart, but also our heavenly Father's heart.

—*James Robison*
Founder and President, LIFE Outreach International
Fort Worth, Texas

In an era of knee-jerk reactions and an overabundance of opinions, ideologies, and political partisanship, Bishop Harry Jackson's voice cuts to the core of what matters most with thoughtful, well-researched, and experience-based solutions that are desperately needed for the times we are living in today.

—*Jentezen Franklin*
Senior Pastor, Free Chapel
New York Times Best-Selling Author

Bishop Jackson's *A Manifesto* is a beacon of hope, and a clear roadmap to repentance, healing, and restoration for our times.

—*Evangelist Alveda C. King*
Alveda King Ministries

a huge heart. *A Manifesto: Christian America's Contract with Minorities* is a book at the right time and for the right reasons. It provides a strategy on how to strengthen our nation through building bridges as we listen to one another. Most of all, Bishop Jackson urges us to have the courage to be a servant leader as we strive to create a more perfect union.

—*Dr. Jay H. Strack*
President, Student Leadership University

In his book, *A Manifesto: Christian America's Contract with Minorities*, Bishop Harry R. Jackson Jr. rightly incorporates *wealth creation* through home ownership as a key component of the "EMPOWERED" acrostic. The pursuit of a Promised Land is a central Old Testament theme and "house churches" birthed the New Testament church. Christian home ownership is, in fact, an essential manifestation of American values and freedoms.

—*Don F. Harris, Esq.*
Senior Advisor, UHOUSI Initiative

The so-called doctrine of *the separation of church and state* has always been a myth. Our founding fathers never wanted the benefits of a strong, Christian culture to be removed from the public sphere—yet that's exactly what has happened. And the result has been across-the-board lapses in morality that threaten to destroy what's left of our society. But Bishop Harry Jackson's *A Manifesto: Christian America's Contract with Minorities* offers a solution that will bring about the changes we desperately need.

—*Dr. Thomas D. Mullins*
Founding Pastor, Christ Fellowship Church

HARRY R. JACKSON, JR.

A MANIFESTO

CHRISTIAN AMERICA'S
CONTRACT WITH MINORITIES

WHITAKER
HOUSE

A MANIFESTO
Christian America's Contract with Minorities

Harry R. Jackson Jr.
Harry Jackson Ministeries
6251 Ammendale Road
Beltsville, MD 20705
www.harryjacksonministries.com

ISBN: 978-1-64123-566-2
eBook ISBN: 978-1-64123-567-9
Printed in the United States of America
© 2020 by Harry R. Jackson Jr.

Whitaker House
1030 Hunt Valley Circle
New Kensington, PA 15068
www.whitakerhouse.com

Library of Congress Cataloging-in-Publication Data (Pending)

1 2 3 4 5 6 7 8 9 10 11 ᴜᴊ 27 26 25 24 23 22 21 20

CONTENTS

CHAPTER 1

SHARED DESTINY

When I was about eight years old, my family began taking me and my brother Eric on long trips from Cincinnati, Ohio, to Norfolk, Virginia. It's easily a nine- to eleven-hour drive. The roads and the terrain changed frequently, and so did our drivers to ensure the stress of the trip wasn't on one person alone.

Bathroom and food breaks were numerous, but we always arrived early in the evening, before sunset. We were joyfully greeted by Big Mama, our aunts, and scores of cousins and friends. Those summers were amazing. The food, fun, and fellowship were unparalleled.

My parents often drove back home after reconnecting with our huge extended family for only thirty-six hours, leaving me and Eric in Virginia for six to eight weeks annually. Those wonderful vacations enabled me and my brother to learn our family's narrative and aspirations, as well as where all *the bodies* were buried. To its credit, our family produced a chief justice on the Supreme Court of Virginia, nurses who ran city-wide departments, school principals, social workers, teachers, college professors, military personnel, FBI agents, real estate agents, and a few preachers.

In many ways, America today resembles my family back then. We need to think about minorities as being the precocious, ever-maturing children of a large family who are rapidly growing up. As they do so, they can help to drive our country to a better destination. Our goal for every minority group is full participation and full ownership of our values and the rights and privileges of our land.

A MANIFESTO FOR SOCIAL CHANGE

This book will set forth a biblical agenda or manifesto for social change in our nation. Christians of every denomination and ethnic stripe will be welcomed into our new coalition to add their proportional contribution to our national vision and strategic direction. We will continue to use the metaphor of a family traveling together in order to describe what we have to do to arrive at our family's destination safely and in good spirits.

Let me explain: most Christians believe that they have been invited into a fully functioning family. As we live out our values in the marketplace, we are called to influence the world in which we live.

For years, secular humanists and nonbelievers from every walk of life have been telling the church and its members to retreat back within the walls of our houses of worship. They have attempted to give us only freedom of worship within the walls of the church, without freedom to express our beliefs and lifestyle outside those walls.

The mythic doctrine called the separation of church and state has been both misunderstood and misapplied.

The mythic doctrine called *the separation of church and state* has been both misunderstood and misapplied. Our founders wanted to protect the church from government control. Instead, many anti-church crusaders envision an unfounded right to control the church's engagement in secular conversations about law, public policy, and culture.

I have written this work because the church is no longer living in our grandmothers' America. The *moral majority* can no longer be defined as a group of aging white men with ironclad influence over its church members' thoughts, lifestyles, and social practices.

In 2018, William H. Frey's research clearly indicated that the U.S. would become "minority white" within the next twenty or twenty-five years. His statistics also point out that for youth, the post-millennial minority population under eighteen is expected to become the majority in 2020. The browning of America will be received with joy by many and fear by others. This demographic changes will affect fashion, industry, our engagement with media, and hundreds of nuances concerning how we live, love, and express ourselves in the years ahead.

Anyone who watches cable news or peruses social media will acknowledge the fact that both generational and ethnic tensions are rising. Frey makes a surprising declaration in his book, Diversity Explosion: How New Racial Demographics are Remaking America. He says, "The current period of profound racial change will lead to a less-divided nation than today's older whites or younger minorities fear." [1]

How will such change be beneficial and unifying for America? And how will it help minorities? Obviously culture, music, and fashion will change as time and taste move forward. These demographic changes will also affect politics and political power.

As things are heating up for the 2020 elections and beyond, many political observers, including at least three major polling organizations, are reporting a surprising shift of African American voters away from the Democratic party. A similar trend is occurring among Hispanic and Asian voters as well. What's driving these changes? And if the predictions are correct, what will this mean for the minority communities and for the nation as a whole?

These are exactly the questions I am poised to address. But in order to do so, I must use a group of foundational moral, spiritual, and political assumptions, as well as some historical background, to give you the answers.

The first principle is that comparable belief systems and world views will produce unity. The Bible says, "How can two walk together unless they agree?" (See Amos 3:3.) Values agreement is a part of every premarital counseling process I'm aware of. Therefore, we are poised to see a minority demographic shift that, if followed by a unifying values shift, will produce a positive political vote shift.

TWO TERRIBLE BUMPS ON OUR JOURNEY

This winter and spring, two incredible moral bumps in the road have appeared that may affect our journey and must be included in our manifesto. The first bump in the road is the COVID-19 pandemic. The second bump is the terrible murders and public deaths of Ahmaud Arbery, Breonna Taylor, and George Floyd, and the protests and rioting that followed.

Let's begin with the murders of blacks like George Floyd and others while in police custody. From the beginning, I advised the White House and the administration that Floyd's murder in Minneapolis would erupt into another wave of riots like those that occurred after the death of Michael Brown Jr. in Ferguson, Missouri, in 2014. I advised both President Trump and Vice President Pence to address two separate messages to the nation. The first message primarily addressed to blacks that the administration feels their pain and will keep them safe, even when in police custody. The second message on law and order, I advised them, should be tempered because so-called law-and-order politicians from the 1950s onward were often anti-black. This message *must* include specific police reform changes as well.

My comments and suggestions are a part of the public record in the vice presidential listening session at my church in Maryland and the presidential listening session a week later in Dallas, Texas.

Collectively, the entire Christian community must speak to the hearts of minorities and say, "We love you, we cherish you, and there is a place for you in this land."

There is a full bodied history that is not known by most Christians. This book must be put in the hands of Christians of all ethnicities. Largely, this generation's whites feel shamed or blamed, instead of realizing that although they did not cause these race problems, they have been entrusted with a divine moment in which they can make dramatic progress in healing the racial divide. Collectively, the entire Christian community must speak to the hearts of blacks and other minorities. We must say, "We love you, we cherish you, and there is a place for you in this land." Only Christians can heal the racial divide because we can truly speak heart to heart. I am recommending that a national prayer movement be ignited by the Reconciled Church movement and other allied prayer initiatives.

Many conservative whites don't seem to realize that blacks forty years old and under are engaged in protests because they are only six or seven generations away from slavery in which blacks were lynched and tortured.

SENATE APOLOGY FOR LYNCHINGS

I was in a closed-door session with five other national black leaders and U.S. Senator Bill Frist from Tennessee as he presented the concepts of Senate Resolution 39 of the 109th Congress, Apologizing to Lynching Victims and Their Descendants, which was signed into law in June 2005. Here is an excerpt of that historic legislation:

> Whereas the crime of lynching succeeded slavery as the ultimate expression of racism in the United States following Reconstruction; whereas lynching was a widely acknowledged practice in the United States until the middle of the 20th century; whereas lynching was a crime that occurred throughout the United States, with documented incidents in all but 4 States; whereas at least 4,742 people, predominantly

African-Americans, were reported lynched in the United States between 1882 and 1968; whereas 99 percent of all perpetrators of lynching escaped from punishment by State or local officials; whereas lynching prompted African-Americans to form the National Association for the Advancement of Colored People (NAACP) and prompted members of B'nai B'rith to found the Anti-Defamation League;...

Now, therefore, be it Resolved, That the Senate--

(1) apologizes to the victims of lynching for the failure of the Senate to enact anti-lynching legislation;

(2) expresses the deepest sympathies and most solemn regrets of the Senate to the descendants of victims of lynching, the ancestors of whom were deprived of life, human dignity, and the constitutional protections accorded all citizens of the United States; and

(3) remembers the history of lynching, to ensure that these tragedies will be neither forgotten nor repeated.

WHY POLICE BRUTALITY HITS HOME

For blacks and other minorities, brutality and death in police custody is the new lynching. They feel as though these acts are the height of dehumanization.

I wish I had branded an alternative phrase to Black Lives Matter years ago. I would have simply rephrased it to *Black People's Lives Count* or *All Black Lives Matter*.

Unfortunately, many conservative whites begin to compare the black deaths over a weekend in Chicago with the number of blacks who die at the hands of the police in urban areas. Often, blacks feel that this kind of analysis is not genuine. It's a game of *blame the victim*. It's not an apples to apples comparison. Black abortions matter, black urban murders matter, black over-incarceration matters (the new Jim Crow laws), black under-education matters, black fatherlessness matters, and black wealth matters.

Many frustrated African Americans say that every time we accumulate wealth, the white power brokers take it away from us. They cite the massacre at the Black Wall Street near Tulsa in 1921. In that incident alone, one hundred and fifty to three hundred black men were killed or lynched, and their businesses and homes were razed to the ground.

The history and strategies set forth in this book encompass my humble attempt to shine a light in the darkness. From the treehouse to the house on Elm Street, there must be biblical clarity. From the ghetto to the White House, there must be moral authority. From the slums to the suburbs, there must be a way up the socioeconomic ladder.

UNITY OF THOUGHT CREATES ADVANCEMENT

I played on a state championship football team made up of blacks and whites, but we competed in a part of my state that was very racist and filled with Ku Klux Klan followers. I remember the team bus pulling up to a school fifty miles outside of Cincinnati, Ohio, the town in which I was raised. There were signs saying that blacks were not allowed. These crude signs actually used the graphic "N" word. The crowd carrying the signs was loud, rude, and filled with hate-filled rhetoric.

My team was comprised of undersized, rich, white kids with one outsized black kid—me. We exited the bus despite the challenge of the crowd. By the end of the game, we had won by a margin of over fifty points. That's right—fifty points.

Clear game strategies and excellent conditioning allowed us to defeat mean-spirited teams of all stripes. We overcame stereotypes and physically superior individual athletes.

Our team won because of hard work in practices and a unified strategy executed under the watchful eye of a visionary coach. We were undefeated two years in a row and became first place in our division my senior year.

Minorities in America have the same kind of opportunity that my high school football team had. Believe it or not, we can unite, strategize, and help advance the nation...if we come together. The major question is, who will be the coach? Who will lead the way?

We need a cadre of leaders who rise up in the spirit of Dr. Martin Luther King Jr. Of necessity, they have to be multi-ethnic, self-sacrificing, and insightful enough to anticipate the future.

During the civil rights movement, black clergy courageously led the way. They believed that a media event would be used by the Holy Spirit to convict the majority culture of non-Christian standards and values. They believed that all Americans believed in the high-sounding goals and vision articulated in both the Bible and the nation's Constitution. They sought to reform the American culture and cause a *civil revival* that reached far beyond the church house into the streets, the homes, and the hearts of the individual citizens of the nation.

Black reformers cannot lead national change alone. Today, we must add the interests of Hispanic, Asian, and other young adult voters' concerns. The nation's Christian faith and common sense are still our greatest unifiers. In the first Great Awakening that swept across our thirteen colonies between the 1730s and 1740s, there was an emphasis on personal spiritual renewal that produced societal change at a grassroots level. This movement almost singlehandedly promoted the ideas of human dignity, equality, and the abolition of slavery. This revival movement permanently transformed Protestantism and the emerging U.S. culture. Minorities must no longer see ourselves as victims but victors who will raise the level of biblical righteousness and justice in America.

Minorities must no longer see ourselves as victims but victors who will raise the level of biblical righteousness and justice in America.

In this hour of social media, smart phones, and selfies, a grassroots movement may be easier than ever to kindle and maintain. All we lack are leaders armed with a manifesto, a new coalition of spiritual leaders who are held together by common sense, biblical values, and a set of easy-to-accomplish political goals that can once again *awaken* America.

This work outlines a nine-point moral and political agenda that can be used to unite the hearts, minds, and values of our nation's minorities. Naturally, able men and women must hear the call and rise to lead.

This manifesto can easily be remembered through an acrostic using the word *empowered.*

EMPOWERED

+ Education Reform
+ Marriage Rebuilding as a Social Strategy
+ Public Policy Reform
+ Oversight of Minority and Community Engagement
+ Wealth Creation
+ Entrepreneurship
+ Righteousness and Justice as Moral Guidelines
+ Empathy versus Retaliation
+ Destiny with Dignity for All Humankind

Let's address these nine points, one by one. Our goal in becoming *empowered* is to benefit our culture and refashion our society on the anvil of solid Christian truth. This can be the ultimate win-win as opposed to a carnal power grab. There is more than enough division and polarization going on.

Education Reform

Education reforms have been attempted by the last few presidential administrations. These have seemed to lurch back and forth, resulting in surface changes only. Studies repeatedly show a gap between majority and minority reading and math levels by the third grade. What is needed today is an educational solution that will level the playing field.

Past education reforms have seemed to lurch back and forth, resulting in surface changes only.

America seeks to be a meritocracy, with a government run by people based on their talents and abilities rather than their ancestry or wealth. Education properly dispensed can create such a society.

During my forty years as a pastor, I have seen minorities sacrifice for the next generation by sending their children to private or religious schools. My own father sent me to the excellent Cincinnati Country Day School, Williams College, and Harvard Business School. He and my mother, an elementary school teacher, believed that climbing the educational ladder was essential for blacks to mainstream and overcome barriers of advancement.

Some Necessary Reforms

Here are some necessary public reforms to improve our educational system:

+ Charter schools
+ Private religious and character-based education through third grade
+ After-school and faith-based tutorial centers located in churches
+ Mentoring programs for college-bound minority males because of high dropout rates

- Religious-based thirteenth year programs
- Military service and trade school training for kids who are not college-bound
- Public policies and grants developed for effective Christian schools
- Encouragement of minority kids to pursue advanced and professional school degrees

Marriage Rebuilding as a Social Strategy

Churches must work with families to create a marriage culture.

Public Policy Reform

There are three dimensions of public policies that minorities must continue to advocate for.

Criminal Justice Reform

The First Step Act, signed into law by President Trump on December 21, 2018, must be continued. According to the Board of Prisons, the act was designed "to reduce the size of the federal prison population while also creating mechanisms to maintain public safety." The six major areas the Bureau of Prison (BOP) highlights as the achievements of the First Step Act are:

1. **Reduction in Recidivism**

2. **Incentives for Success** (good time credit for every year)

3. **Confinement** (provision to house inmates within 500 driving miles of their residence)

4. **Correctional Reforms**

These include: prohibition on the use of restraints on pregnant inmates in the custody of BOP and the U.S. Marshals

Service; a requirement for the BOP "to provide tampons and sanitary napkins that meet industry standards to prisoners for free and in a quantity that meets the health care needs of each prisoner"; and prohibition against the use of solitary confinement for juvenile delinquents in federal custody. BOP does not house juveniles in its facilities but its contracts comply with this aspect of the First Step Act.

5. Sentencing Reforms

This includes changes to mandatory minimum sentences for certain drug offenders. The First Step Act made the provisions of the Fair Sentencing Act of 2010 (P.L. 111-220) retroactive so that currently incarcerated offenders who received longer sentences for possession of crack cocaine versus powder cocaine can submit a petition in federal court to have their sentences reduced.

6. Expanding the Safety Valve

The act also expands the safety valve provision, which allows courts to sentence low-level, nonviolent drug offenders with minor criminal histories to less than the required mandatory minimum for an offense.

The act requires the submission of several reports to review the BOP's implementation of the law and assess the effects of the new risk and needs assessment system.

Oversight of Minority and Community Engagement

This area speaks of the need for specific strategic engagement in the local political process. Minority participation on platform committees and at political conventions will be essential for true political empowerment. Currently, minority opinions are simply ignored because of a lack of participation. The kind of leadership needed here is less like charismatic Dr.

King and more like political action committees, regional get-out-the-vote efforts, and a myriad of tactical approaches to political engagement.

Wealth Creation

The foundational building block of personal wealth in the U.S. is home ownership. An apartment dweller only transfers a few thousand dollars to the next generation. Homeowners, however, pass on more than $150,000 of next generation equity. Black home ownership was at a 42 percent level in 2017, according to the Urban Institute. The gap between black and white home ownership that year was 30 percent.

Interestingly, the home ownership gap between blacks and whites in the U.S. is bigger today than it was in 1960, when 38 percent of blacks and 65 percent of whites owned homes. In those days, it was legal to discriminate and to refuse to sell homes to minorities in certain communities. It's a shame that in the decades since the passage of the 1968 Fair Housing Act, this wealth gap still exists.

According to the National Association of Hispanic Real Estate Professionals, the Hispanic home ownership rate in 2017 was 46.2 percent, just a bit higher than the rate for the black community. Asians, however, had home ownership rates comparable to whites. Nonetheless, they do not have equal access. "Many Asian households tend to live in multigenerational households at a higher rate, and it shows up as a higher homeownership rate," explains Gary Painter, a public policy professor at the University of South California. [2]

Additionally, the 2017 American Community Survey reported that Asian homeowners are often required to pay higher down payments than other ethnic groups—sometimes as high as 35 percent.

Entrepreneurship

When I was growing up, older blacks told stories about the number of black businesses that existed in their community. Unfortunately, as segregation shrank, it seems that the celebration of black businesses also shrank. My grandfather was raised knowing how to farm and quit school after the second grade. After he moved from South Carolina to Cincinnati, Ohio, he started a construction business that gave about twenty-five people a sense of purpose and mission in life, along with a pay check. After he became a Christian, he led his business according to the principles of the Word of God. Our minority community needs millions of business leaders who can serve their communities in like manner.

Our minority community needs millions of business leaders who can serve their communities guided by the Word of God.

According to the 2015 U.S. Census, there were 8 million minority-owned businesses in the United States. The 21st-century question for minority businesses is, "How many of these entities see themselves as instruments of social change?" And a follow-up question could be, "Can U.S. minorities follow the example of the Republic of Israel, which is the international leader of startup businesses, despite centuries' long discrimination?"

It will take major changes in funding and venture capital resources to fuel the growth of small businesses with an international vision. Job creation and community revitalization can be achieved through the growth and prosperity of minority businesses. Both political parties must be challenged to offer greenhouse programs that will aid in the planting and development of such growth.

Righteousness and Justice as Moral Guidelines

In late 2004, I burst onto the national scene as a social commentator. At that time, I was one of the few black conservatives who were featured on cable news networks. I began to realize then that the Christian community was deeply divided on their political engagement based on a simple paradigm.

The Christian community is divided into two camps: those seeking biblical justice and those advocating for righteousness.

As black Christians, we're very interested in biblical justice, advocacy for the poor, and ministry to the disadvantaged in our culture. Some social scientists have even gone so far as to declare that minorities cannot be racists because of their lack of power, position, and generational wealth.

White evangelicals, on the other hand, have consistently advocated for what I call righteousness issues that involve personal responsibility. These include traditional marriage, the rights of the unborn, and seeking prohibitions on things like gambling.

I realized that the Bible actually presents both righteousness and justice issues as valid moral concerns. My eyes were opened to the fact that the nation needed a balance of morally engaged citizens who saw things through both lenses—righteousness and justice. In fact, I began to proclaim the words of Psalm 89:14–17:

> *Righteousness and justice are the foundation of your throne; love and faithfulness go before you. Blessed are those who have learned to acclaim you, who walk in the light of your presence, LORD. They rejoice in your name all day long; they celebrate your righteousness. For you are their glory and strength, and by your favor you exalt our horn.*

Mature Christians should advocate both for life for the unborn and criminal justice reform. We should care for widows and orphans and also protect traditional heterosexual marriage.

Empathy versus Retaliation

At the Congressional prayer breakfast on February 6, 2020, I sat as one of nearly 4,000 participants from 120 nations and heard a powerful prophetic message from Arthur C. Brooks. He is a devout believer, conservative thought leader, and author of a book entitled *Love Your Enemies.* [3] His speech called for outrageous, Christ-like love to invade our personal, public, and political arenas.

Unfortunately, most of the audience, myself included, was thinking about how much their family, friends, and enemies needed to hear this word. Many Sunday mornings, we sit in judgment of others while nursing our personal wounds, instead of applying the Scriptures to ourselves.

As an African American, I have often been guilty of pointing my self-righteous, accusing forefinger at others. I often forget that there are more fingers pointing back at me than I point at others. All minorities, especially blacks, will have to exercise forgiveness in order to find personal healing and healing of our nation's public wounds and sins.

Perhaps one of the most needed arenas of forgiveness is the area of ethnic tensions. In Matthew 24, Jesus says that in the last days, ethnic groups will rise up against each other in real tribal war. Only the church has the ability to rise above the cultural rifts of gender, class, and ethnicity. The great apostle Paul states this truth: *"There is neither Jew nor Gentile, neither slave nor free, nor is there male and female, for you are all one in Christ Jesus"* (Galatians 3:28).

Destiny with Dignity for All Humankind

Made in the image and likeness of God in our moral, spiritual, and intellectual essence, all of us have the right to fulfill our destinies with dignity. Endowed with unique characteristics bestowed on us by our Creator, it's within our nature to act in accordance with His will, which is to choose good over evil, to love Him and each other.

GETTING TO OUR DESTINATION

Now that we have articulated our Christian manifesto, we must start the process of getting everyone on the same page concerning our destination. Where do we want our American culture to land? Do we want to be a socialistic country or a capitalistic nation? What should be the financial opportunities? What should health care look like?

These are destiny questions. As a child, I never realized that the reason my family took us to Norfolk each summer was a rite of passage. They wanted us to relate to our highly motivated and close-knit family. They chose Norfolk because our matriarch and patriarch lived there: Big Mama and my grandfather Reverend Davis.

Reverend Davis was a joyful former prizefighter with arms as big as some men's legs. When we stayed in his house during the summer, every Sunday was a mixture of joyful worship at the country church he pastored and joyful family fellowship over the weekly feast called Sunday dinner. I can still smell the hot buttered rolls and sweet potato pie. And I remember the stories, the discussions, and the prayers that we shared around the table. These times helped me become more than a Cincinnati ghetto dweller. I became a full-fledged Jackson as I spent time in Norfolk. My summer eventually affected my destiny. If we had stayed in Cincinnati every summer, I would have become a different person.

So the next question we Christians have to ask ourselves is, "Where do we want to train our growing family?" It's time to choose the location of our family vacation. What spiritual, political, and social destination do we wish to reach? In this generation, Christian leaders must write a new Christian manifesto or declaration of values. People like Francis Schaeffer, James Dobson, Chuck Colson, Billy Graham, and host of others produced seminal works in years gone by. The EMPOWERED acrostic is simply my attempt to create a new understanding of vision.

Christians must remember that we have a shared destiny, but in the next chapter, we need to decide where we are going to spend our summers. We need to decide what our family's values are going to be and what it means to be an engaged believer in the generations to come.

CHAPTER 2

SHARED DESTINATION—A TIME FOR CHANGE

Over the years of our traveling to Norfolk, my brother and I learned many great things, and I established important habits and rituals. One year, we got the unfortunate news that our grandfather, the gregarious Rev. Davis, had died. He had suffered a massive heart attack while running up to the pulpit as he normally did. That summer, we had to stay at a different home. I vaguely remember that everything had changed. Eventually, we moved to a different house for most of the summer. In fact, I remember three different *headquarter homes*, each of which had advantages and disadvantages, fun times and sad times. Our destiny was indelibly shaped by the trips, but the destination had to change as our family dynamic had changed.

Our American culture is changing, too—and it's time to recognize that. We need to create a new principle-based coalition to change the direction of our personal lives, our communities, and our nation. Many of us long for the truths of Scripture to be sown into the foundation of our culture once again. We don't just want dry religious practices; we want the living faith of our elders. We want a fresh experience with

God that affects our everyday lives. Black, whites, Hispanics, Asians, and millennials must come together in order to be *empowered*.

I'd like to share a little black cultural history that shows how difficult it is for a group to change destinations. Please remember that the lessons I am expounding upon apply to all minority cultural and political resets.

Old habits die hard. As most folks know, that old axiom is painfully true. How many times have you tried to change a thought, a behavior, or a routine of some kind and found out that unless you really focus on it and work at it, you just keep doing the same old things over and over? I suspect everybody over the age of twenty-one knows exactly what I'm talking about. We want to change, but there are plenty of us who keep on doing things we'd rather not do, even when we realize that certain habits can be counterproductive or even destructive. The apostle Paul certainly understood this problem.

> *"I have the right to do anything," you say—but not every-thing is beneficial.* (1 Corinthians 6:12)

For more than seventy years, the Democratic Party has been the party of choice in the African American community. The Civil Rights Act of 1964, enacted by President Lyndon B. Johnson's administration, galvanized millions of black voters into an engaged and outspoken community of socially and politically active citizens, and the party was there to welcome us aboard.

Johnson's deeper motivations, his vulgarity, and his racist attitude were generally overlooked because our people had finally achieved a measure of recognition for the abuses and indignities we had endured for so long. We now had strong legislation on our side, and we believed we were standing at the threshold of a social and political revolution.

Suddenly, our voices and our values mattered. Democratic politicians were eager to gain our trust, and they came by the dozens. White candidates knew almost nothing about our community, but they pledged undying devotion and promised us the moon. Even though African Americans made up fewer than 13 percent of the population and a much lower percentage of the voting public, our votes mattered. Our votes could determine the outcome of a close election—and they still can. So the die was cast; before long, the whole world knew that African Americans would cast their votes for anybody with a "D" after their name, without really thinking about what that person really stood for, or had ever done for the black community.

Before long, pulling the Democrat lever on Election Day was an ingrained habit. Anyone who dared to question the loyalty or truthfulness of the Democratic candidates or, heaven forbid, actually vote for a Republican, was suddenly an outcast...or worse. We had learned the importance of a unified voice in the presidential elections of the 1950s, along with the risks of betting on unpopular candidates. In 1952, 76 percent of the black vote went for the Democratic candidate, Adlai Stevenson. In the rematch four years later, Stevenson got 61 percent of the black vote. In both cases, Stevenson lost to the popular war hero and Republican rival, Gen. Dwight D. Eisenhower. Even with those large percentages, there were simply too few black votes to affect the outcome.

Black votes were often sketchy and unpredictable in the first half of the last century, but as the distinguished author and journalist Chuck Stone pointed out, that would change dramatically after the election of 1960, when African

Americans united to give John F. Kennedy 70 percent of their votes. In his review of the cultural dynamics in that election, published in 1977, Stone said, "One of the axioms of black electoral behavior holds that a cohesive black vote controls the balance of power in national elections." [4] However, he noted, certain conditions must be met for that to happen.

Many observers attributed JFK's razor's edge election victory to the black vote. The axiom that black votes determine who wins, however, "presumes three conditions: (1) the white vote must split almost 50-50; (2) blacks must swing at least 75% of their votes to the winning candidate; and (3) either the winning candidate or a respected authority must publicly acknowledge the debt. [5]

Kennedy won with almost universal black support, and the Republican national chairman at the time, Thruston Morton, admitted that the black vote gave Kennedy the edge over his Republican rival, Richard Nixon. Sixteen years later, Jimmy Carter would receive an astonishing 92 percent of the black vote, which was surprising for many reasons, but his gratitude was slow in coming. Stone writes, "Jimmy Carter, at best a cautious integrationist, at worst a subcutaneous segregationist, waited 27 days until he could muster sufficient courage to thank publicly blacks for their axial role in his victory. And at that, he did it by telephone." [6]

It was the height of irony that the descendants of black slaves sent a Georgia redneck to the White House. The 1976 election gave blacks a strong, viable political platform and an undeniable impact for decades to come. But Carter and the Democratic Party paid for their disrespect and lack of gratitude in 1980. Although 83 percent of black voters stuck with Carter, 14 percent voted for the former actor and California governor, Ronald Reagan.

EXPANDING INFLUENCE

To his credit, Reagan was aware of the importance of a unified national electorate. His Hollywood experience may have taught him that. His films dealt with universal themes and appealed to a large, diverse audience. But during each of his political campaigns, Reagan emphasized the importance of reaching out to minority voters and expanding the Republican tent. Confronted by a wide range of domestic and foreign challenges at the time, he called for a unified voice to address issues of concern to all Americans, especially including the concerns of African Americans.

Major events such as the Selma riots, the emerging civil rights movement, and the assassination of Dr. Martin Luther King Jr. made it very clear that things would have to change. In a speech delivered on January 15, 1977, just five days before Jimmy Carter took the oath of office, Reagan said, "The New Republican party I envision is still going to be the party of Lincoln and that means we are going to have to come to grips with what I consider to be a major failing of the party: its failure to attract the majority of black voters. It's time black America and the New Republican party move toward each other and create a situation in which no black vote can be taken for granted." [7]

Reagan believed his party could win a substantial percentage of the black vote in 1980, and he made the point again in his speech to the Urban League in New York on August 5, 1980, when he said, "I am committed to the protection and enforcement of the civil rights of black Americans. This commitment is interwoven into every phase of the programs I will propose." [8]

Reagan's campaign stalled out in 1976, due in part to scurrilous attacks from the left, but President Carter's political blunders, the gasoline shortages, oppressive taxes, growing pessimism, a widespread malaise among the public, and, ultimately the Iran Hostage Crisis, damaged the Democrats too badly and gave Reagan the margin he needed for back-to-back victories in 1980 and 1984. Although Reagan received 14 percent of the black vote in 1980, that dropped to 9 percent in 1984 while his opponent, Walter Mondale, garnered 91 percent. But the Democrat brand had been tarnished; with 86 percent of white votes going to Reagan that year, he won his second term by a landslide, sweeping forty-nine states.

Since 1992, no candidate has won the Democratic nomination for president without winning a majority of the black vote. Bill Clinton received 70 percent of the black vote that year and 84 percent in 1996. But once again, it wasn't enough. Clinton's endless string of social, political, and sexual misdeeds would crater the Democrats' election hopes for two election cycles. Until Barack Obama appeared on the scene and was elected as America's first black president—a term Clinton once claimed for himself—no Democratic candidate could gain enough traction to stop the Republicans.

Obama owned the black vote for both of his terms. By 2016, African Americans made up 24 percent of Democratic primary voters, which was the most ever recorded. With that advantage, Hillary Clinton won the nomination and went on to win 77 percent of the black vote in the general election, trailing only slightly the 82 percent that Obama had received in 2008. Yet despite the almost universal belief that she would destroy her billionaire Republican opponent in November, she lost.

CONFLICT AND CONTROVERSY

Perhaps no political loss in history has caused such a wave of national and international turmoil. As I will discuss further in the pages that follow, no American presidential candidate has ever endured such visceral hatred that has been levied against President Donald J. Trump, who narrowly lost the popular vote but won the Electoral College by a vote of 304 to 227. We are, of course, still very much in the crucible of these events, immersed in a war of words and a politically hostile environment like nothing I have ever seen in my lifetime.

As we approach November 2020, the tensions and risks are as great as ever. While prior elections have generally shown a united black voice favoring Democratic candidates, there is increasing evidence that this solid base of support could be fracturing. Writing in *The Hill* in October 2019, political journalist Jonathan Easley said a surprising number of black political journalists, strategists, and academics have concluded that the 2020 presidential election will be a game-changer. Democratic frontrunner Joe Biden "has his arms around African American support and is squeezing ever tighter in these communities, particularly among older black voters," said Antjuan Seawright, a Democratic strategist in South Carolina. "But anyone around this business knows that things can change in a twinkle of an eye." [9]

Even suggesting a change of this magnitude has Democratic strategists up in arms. The Democrat-controlled Congress and left-leaning national media have worked day and night to discredit and demean the sitting president. They've impeached him, reviled him, and leveled every accusation they can think of at him, yet somehow, President Trump continues to outflank his adversaries, gaining a massive wave of support from regular Americans of all racial and political backgrounds.

His endless string of coast-to-coast rallies, relaunched in June 2020 after an easing of COVID-19 restrictions, are populated by Americans of every class, color, and creed.

With such an incredible history of black allegiance to the Democratic Party over more than six decades, we have to wonder: is it even remotely possible that a majority of black voters would turn out to support the Republican candidate in November? As it turns out, some of the men and women making the most surprising predictions for that possibility are prominent voices within the black community. Among them is Bob Johnson, founder and CEO of the BET Television Network, who said in a televised interview that the Democrats do not have a candidate who can beat Donald Trump in November:

> I think the president has always been in a position where it's his to lose based on his bringing a sort of disruptive force into what would be called political norms. I don't care if it's the way he conducts foreign policy, the way he takes on government agencies, and the way he deals with immigration, he brings his style. Now, a lot of people, particularly those who voted for him and those who will vote for him again in the next election, like that style. I think what the Democrats have to do is to be careful to not get caught up in sty-listic-Trump and more in substantive-Trump. [10]

In the fall of 2019, prior to the economic troubles related to COVID-19, Johnson noted Trump had done "positive things" for the economy:

> For African Americans, the trend continues to be favorable. There used to be an old saying, "When white America catches a cold, African Americans get

pneumonia." It's going the opposite way now. White unemployment is going down, African American unemployment is going down. That's a plus-plus that you can't argue with. I give the president credit for doing positive things, when I see a president doing positive things, particularly for African Americans. [11]

All of that, combined with the commander-in-chief's "style," Johnson said, makes the 2020 election "his to lose." But Johnson isn't the only one speaking in such terms. In an op-ed article published on Election Day in 2016, United Nations ambassador and former NFL star Jack Brewer cited research from the Cook Political Report affirming the growing importance of the black vote…along with a caveat.

"The black vote made such an impact that in 2012," he said, "it accounted for Obama's entire margin of victory in seven states, including Florida, Maryland, Michigan, Nevada, Ohio, Pennsylvania and Virginia." [12] But as impressive as that was, Brewer pointed to three critical factors that could cause large numbers of blacks to sit out the 2016 election, and he accurately predicted that Donald Trump would be the de facto winner on Election Day.

Those three factors, Brewer said, were: jobs, with the black unemployment rate then at nearly 9 percent or twice that of whites; education, with blacks accounting for 34 percent of the high school freshmen held back and 42 percent of students receiving out-of-school suspensions; and trust. Of the latter, Brewer noted:

Under President Bill Clinton and supported by Hillary, more blacks were thrown in prison for non-violent crimes than at any other time in U.S. history. President Clinton also went on to enforce mandatory minimum punishment rules that still today are putting a dagger into many lower and middle class black families. [13]

Honesty, morality, and compassion are important character traits, and they are among the qualities we ought to expect in anyone elected to public office. But many like Brewer have expressed concern about the lack of these and other essential characteristics in their party's platform. An apparent disregard for meaningful prison reform could be indicative of that.

This may be one reason why the popular African American comedian Dave Chappelle shocked a New York audience by admitting he had voted for Hillary Clinton in 2016, but he "didn't feel good" about it, explaining, "She's not right and we all know she's not right." [14]

FAITH AND MORAL CHARACTER

In accord with these observations, several recent polls have shown that black voters are increasingly open to new and better options. Journalist P. R. Lockhart wrote:

> Since the 1990s, black voters have largely backed the candidate that has gone on to win the Democratic nomination, cementing the group's status as powerful players in presidential politics. But that does not mean black voters are a monolith. [15]

In the fall of 2019, when a crowded field was running for president on the Democratic ticket, black voters could spread their support among multiple candidates, Lockhart noted. But they needed to do more than shake hands and make promises. "They also must show a clear understanding of black voters, their needs, and their concerns," Lockhart said. [16]

Today's black voters are paying attention to what the candidates are saying—and they're not satisfied with what they're being offered by the party of record. This shows up most notably in the discoveries of three of America's leading pollsters. Apparently Kanye West, Clint Eastwood, Jon Voight, Mike Tyson, Isaiah Washington, Kid Rock, Stacey Dash, Terrell Owens, Dennis Rodman, and other celebrities aren't the only ones on the Trump bandwagon anymore. The polls show that President Trump is gaining the support of black voters above what any Republican president has ever received.

Why? In addition to a strong economy and historically low black unemployment prior to the fallout from COVID-19, Trump has supported minority small businesses, historically black colleges and universities, and passage of criminal justice reform. Additionally, troubling signs of the nation's moral and spiritual decline have led many African Americans to reconsider their options.

As I have been saying for more than two decades, the moral values of black Christians are no longer compatible with the policies and practices of the Democratic Party, which prefers secularism over our traditional Christian faith. In August 2019, the Democratic National Committee unanimously passed a resolution that embraced *religiously unaffiliated* voters, proclaiming that 70 percent of such people vote for Democrats and share their values, such as supporting same-sex marriage. What a damning statement.

What this really means for the party, the resolution states, is that a "targeted outreach" to non-religious Americans has "the potential to deliver millions more votes for Democrats in 2020." [17]

Rightfully, no greater issue separates black Americans from the questionable faith and values of the Democratic Party than the issue of abortion, which is a national tragedy. Of the more than 63 million infants who have been aborted since the infamous *Roe v. Wade* decision of 1973, more than 19 million were the children of African American parents. Today, the abortion rate among blacks is more than three times higher than that of whites. According to a New York City Health Department report released in May 2018, between 2012 and 2016 black mothers in the city terminated 136,426 pregnancies, but gave birth to only 118,127 babies. [18] This means that more than 53 percent of all pregnancies in that four-year span ended in abortion.

Given such stark details, it's really not surprising that *New York Times* columnist Thomas B. Edsall would say that black voters can no longer be taken for granted. He writes:

> The percentage of African-Americans describing themselves as moderate or conservative is almost twice as large as the percentage of white Democratic primary voters who describe themselves that way. [19]

While more than 97 percent of white Democratic voters support abortion on demand in all cases, Edsall reported, one-third of black Democrats said abortion should be illegal. [20]

Nationally, black women terminate pregnancies at far higher rates than other women. In 2014, 36 percent of all abortions were performed on black women. And to illustrate just how false the cry for *reproductive freedom* has been, abortion deaths today far exceed those from cancer, violent crime, heart disease, AIDS, and accidents.

All these factors, taken together, paint a very somber picture and argue for a much deeper level of thought, prayer, and dialogue than we have pursued in the past. They present a formidable challenge to the black church and an even greater challenge to the black community as a whole. What better motivation could we have to change our old allegiances and lift up the banner of a new and imminently worthy cause?

Turning the page, I have to ask: who are we really? What do we believe? Have we traded our birthright, like Esau, for a mess of pottage (see Genesis 25:25–33), or will we speak boldly and clearly about the truths we sincerely believe? I have joined with thousands of concerned Christians and with a growing number of black pastors, ministry leaders, and laymen all over this country in saying, "It's time for a new beginning." Will you join me in that? It's time for African Americans to stand up and speak up for what we truly believe to be true. The black church today is the truest expression of what Christ called His church to be, and this is our hour to proclaim our faith in our homes, in the street, and especially at the polls.

Unfortunately, black activism alone cannot transform the nation quickly enough to avert further traumatic damage to our culture. Blacks must link hands with Hispanics, Asians, and next generation whites to redefine our destination. Where we are today reminds me of one of the later drives we took to Virginia as a family. There was a massive amount of construction work done along our route, but we missed the new detour signs. As a result, my dad overshot our route by about twenty minutes, creating a forty-minute waste of time. This was before the days of our sophisticated GPS systems and programs like that quickly redirect a single family car or a caravan traveling to an important destination. Next, we will look at the humbling process of retracing our steps and rerouting.

CHAPTER 3

REROUTING—A NEW BEGINNING

For some reason, one of the last years we made the trip, we had to deal with patches of new road construction. As a result, we had to adjust to several course corrections. My dad was usually jovial when we were traveling, but he didn't smile about the disruption of his driving plan that time. As I recall, we had gotten a later than normal start. Driving the entire distance during the daylight was not possible this time.

The drive seemed more like an obstacle course. As we redirected for several short *excursions*, he began to tell the family his worst road experiences. The expression *driving while black* had not yet been invented. Nonetheless, he was harassed many times in his long-distance driving ventures. Rerouting sometimes requires more courage than following a familiar path, but upgrading, if done properly, can save time and energy.

The good news is that we finally made it to our destination. The bad news was that my brother and I were more apprehensive than ever about driving at night in rural areas. We learned that every generation needs to pass on its history and values, without sharing paralyzing fears. This is true of the Christian family as well.

Christians in both political parties will tell you, if pressed, that the Bible holds the answers for life's problems. But if that's true, we have to wonder why we as Christians have failed to adhere to the Scripture's command to *"hate evil, love good; establish justice in the gate"* (Amos 5:15 NKJV). There has never been a time when this nation has been so divided. There is war in the streets, war in our hearts, and war in the halls of Congress, where two political parties are doing their best to destroy one another. How in the world have we come to such a pass?

We have failed to teach our children what a biblical worldview looks like, and how to live faithfully according to the principles of our Christian faith.

Part of the problem, no doubt, is the spirit of rebellion that has poisoned so much of the cultural debate in recent years. The founders warned us at the beginning that the idea of liberty would be a dangerous gamble without moral restraint, and we may have fallen into that trap. But an even bigger problem, I believe, is that we have failed to teach our children what a biblical worldview looks like, and how to live faithfully according to the principles of our Christian faith. For at least four generations, young men and women have been denied the moral teachings that could have prevented such a collapse, and the church must bear a share of the blame for that.

The secular worldview that dominates contemporary society is engaged in a constant battle against traditional values, and many in the mainstream culture have little patience for the beliefs that define the Christian church. Nonbelievers scoff at the counsel of Scripture and reject the values and practices of those who name the name of Christ. I suppose some of their fears may be warranted, because even the most sincere Christians are fallible. We say and do things that cause nonbelievers to doubt our motives. But I'm convinced we have the ability to transform the debate through informed engagement, and we have a mandate to show the world a better way.

As we submit our lives to the lordship of Jesus Christ, we have access to a marvelous perspective on life and its demands. The Word of God provides wisdom and guidance for every aspect of our lives, and that includes the rough-and-tumble world of politics. We are not always alert to the needs of others. We focus too much on our own needs and the interests of our loved ones. But Scripture teaches us not only to *"love one another"* (John 13:34), but to *"love your neighbor as yourself"* (Matthew 22:39), which the apostle James calls *"the royal law"* (James 2:8). The challenge now is to put those lessons into practice.

During the 2004 election, a study from the Joint Center for Political and Economic Studies indicated that the number of blacks who would vote for the Republican candidate had doubled since 2000. The reason? A large number of black voters said they were more concerned about moral priorities than political ones. In other words, the Christian moral values espoused by George W. Bush during the campaign meant more to them than the social and political causes exalted by John Kerry and the Democrats in that hotly contested election.

In the 2004 election, the Christian moral values espoused by Bush meant more to black voters than the social and political causes exalted by Kerry.

After that report came out, I spoke about the changing dynamics on national television and said what we call "the new black church" is more like its white counterpart than most of the nation understands. Although the percentage of blacks voting for Bush only increased by a few points, important swing states like Ohio and Florida reported a doubling of black votes since the 2000 election. Fully 16 percent of black voters in Ohio responded positively to the Bush proposals despite the race riots that had taken place there in recent years. At the same time, 13 percent of Florida's black voters went with Bush in 2004, a big increase over the 8 percent he had received in that state in 2000.

Why the change? The answer is that black church leaders in those places were leading their flocks toward a unified Christian front. This was a risky step of faith because there was no clear guarantee that the Republican Party would address the issues black Americans believed to be most important. But these courageous pastors and teachers understood the power of unity, and they believed that there would come a day when the entire body of Christ would come together politically and spiritually. Since that time, many of those leaders have introduced new political and community development paradigms, and new alliances have been formed.

A MOVEMENT OF FAITH

A mature coalition of black and white Christians is absolutely essential if there is any hope of changing the cultural dynamic of the United States. The African American church is one of the most vibrant of all the ethnic sectors in this country. It's no secret why that is true: more than 47 percent of African American adults are born-again Christians. This means that nearly half of the men and women in the black community today are motivated by their Christian faith, and that is bound to have a dramatic impact on the social, cultural, and political life of the nation.

Of course, it will take more than a Christian president to see God's agenda manifested in our country. The men and women who speak for us in the Capitol and in statehouses around the country are there as our representatives. They are there to carry out the "will of the people." But think what that could mean if those people were truly and faithfully committed to carrying out the "will of God." We can never unite around mere ideologies because ideologies will never supplant the Word of God. Our commitment must be to unite around God's truth, follow His leading wherever it may take us, and elect leaders who do likewise.

Our commitment must be to unite around God's truth, follow His leading, and elect leaders who do likewise.

The basis of a biblical political agenda is a commitment to the pursuit of righteousness. In this short statement of principles, I want to lay out a balanced view of God's involvement in the affairs of men. Scripture teaches that righteousness and justice are needed to reflect the glory of God in the earth. Let me put it this way: righteousness is my individual connection with God and my stand before Him. Justice is what I produce for others in the name of God. Righteousness is how I live in the sight of God, while justice is how I begin to release His ability and power on behalf of others.

The light of God's presence will be seen in the United States in an even greater way than ever before as the church learns to move from theology and political ideology into the realm of practice. The Lord desires for this nation to live up to His divine calling, which is a place where personal righteousness motivates leaders to produce justice for the oppressed and needy. Just saying that we pray for those in need every day won't get the job done. The greatest political leaders from now on will be those who help to create a culture that lifts the heavy burdens off the backs of the oppressed by strategic acts of justice, and supports those acts with public policy.

Both conservatives and liberals will need to hear from the minority church; the black church, with experience at social change, must take the lead in tackling the problems of family formation, poverty, and personal freedom. We must also take the lead in redesigning the American dream, so that every citizen will have access to the opportunities and privileges this nation provides. We live in stressful times and we cannot live by the rules of a less fractured time. A new biblical justice movement must come forth to address different social problems than those that existed a half century ago in a cultural landscape that was very different from our own.

The entire body of Christ must vote strategically and make America a greater reflection of God's glory.

The remainder of this book will continue to give the entire body of Christ a coherent way to make a difference. If we chose to *reroute* right now, we will be choosing to make our votes more strategic. We will be choosing to opt for more mainstream political influence. Black, white, Hispanic, and Asian Christians must come together to make America a greater reflection of God's glory. In chapter six, I will lay out seven important, practical issues that should be addressed to heal our ethnic and cultural divisions. In chapter eight, I will delve deeper into the concept of righteousness and justice so that these terms can become lenses through which mature Christians will view the world. This kind of biblical worldview for Christians of all races will enable each person to make a difference in their community.

Before we go on to these monumental topics, however, let me begin by taking you back to a moment that shook the nation and shocked the world.

POLITICAL TRANSFORMATION

Looking back now, we can see that the 2016 presidential election was a major change of direction for America, not simply a transition of governing authority, or a change from one political party to another, but a cultural shift of monumental proportions and a transformation of the political and social framework that will impact this nation for years to come. And the most amazing part was that the Democratic establishment never saw it coming.

For more than two years, every major media outlet, abetted by scores of sophisticated pollsters and political analysts, had assured the world that Hillary Clinton would be America's next president, shattering the glass ceiling for women at the highest levels of government. Polling for *The New York Times* placed Hillary's odds of winning at between 70 and 99 percent. None of their computer models gave the Democrats less than 60 percent of the popular vote. Hillary's victory celebration was a foregone conclusion. The best and brightest would be there to join in the festivities, and the ballroom of New York's Peninsula Hotel on election night was ablaze with lights, music, and enthusiastic revelry as Hillary's fans and supporters swarmed the hall, awaiting the news that their candidate had won in spectacular fashion.

But something unexpected happened. No one wanted to believe it. At first, there were a few whispers, little hints that maybe the pollsters had missed something. Election-night coverage being shown on television screens around the hall was confusing. The numbers coming in from cities and towns across the nation had been showing Hillary with a substantial lead, but suddenly, the momentum began to shift. This was troubling at first, and then deeply disturbing. And the expressions on the faces of Hillary's campaign team only made it worse. What was going on?

Slowly, the noise, the music, and the excitement in the ballroom faded, and one by one, the celebrities and well-wishers disappeared as it became clear that Hillary had lost and the political outsider, the reality-TV star, the New York billionaire every Clinton supporter loved to hate, had won. Campaign organizers Robby Mook and John Podesta did their best to appease the dispirited stragglers, but to no avail. The news would soon be much worse.

As the party ended and the lights went out, Hillary's fans and supporters wandered off in the dark. But as the news spread that Donald J. Trump and the Republican Party had actually won the White House, the crowds of protesters and professional organizers who had waited for hours outside New York's Javits Center took over and unleashed a wave of anger and violence that would enflame several American cities for weeks to come.

THE VOICE OF THE PEOPLE

All of that is history now. We watched it happen, but the controversy and the consequences of the 2016 presidential election will be with us for years. The source of all the anger boiling up on the left was the knowledge that Donald Trump's agenda represented a major shift in the social, political, and cultural direction of the nation. The belief that eight years of the Obama presidency had fundamentally transformed the nation was apparently wrong. And while Democrats were counting on the continuity of the Obama legacy, the unquestioned loyalty of their liberal base, and the predictability of the African American vote, a Republican president would soon be taking the country in a very different direction.

How did this happen? How could the politicians and pundits have been so wrong? The answer is that candidate Trump had been listening to the voice of the people, who were angry, upset with the way the country was going, and calling for a change. With strong support from his conservative base, he began by reaching out and actively courting evangelicals and campaigning in African American communities. He appealed to black Christians through our churches, and promised support not only for our economic concerns, but for our pro-family, pro-life, and faith-based moral values.

Trump promised support for both our economic concerns and our pro-family, pro-life, and faith-based moral values.

During a meeting several years earlier convened by my friend, Pastor Darrell Scott of Ohio, Trump was asked about the claim that he was just another white racist. Trump didn't try to deflect the question, but said, "I am probably the least racist person you know." He said he could never have succeeded in business as he had, working with people of all races and creeds, if he was actually a racist. But what surprised many in the room was that Trump wasn't asking for political support. He said he was asking for their prayers.

He told them he had been meeting with evangelical leaders because he realized he would need godly counsel if he expected to run for the presidency. Darrell said he was impressed that, unlike a lot of people, Trump didn't try to prove he wasn't a racist by saying he had a black friend in the third grade. His friends were the people of all races and backgrounds whom he worked with every day on job sites and in Manhattan boardrooms.

The folks gathering in that room braved the potential rejection of other blacks, but they committed one grave, tactical error. When candidate Trump asked what he could do for blacks as a collective community, they did not have a clear answer. They should have produced a prioritized program for urban renewal, a Marshall Plan-like road map for U.S. urban development.

The Marshall Plan was a strategic initiative passed in 1948 that offered aid to Western Europe. The four-year program dedicated over $12 billion to economic recovery programs after the end of World War II. Our primary goal was to prevent the spread of communism and create prosperous free countries in Europe. The blighted urban communities of America have needed such a plan for years. No one in that meeting produced such a plan. President Trump's Opportunity Zones concept offers the first realistic attempt to tackle urban problems that I have ever seen.

Once Trump actually entered the race for the White House, he expanded his outreach to the black community. I was among a group of pastors invited to meet with him at that time, and while I had my doubts about the man's sincerity at first, I came to see that he genuinely cared about our concerns. I was impressed that he actually listened and responded to what we were saying. He asked for our contact information and said he wanted to stay in touch with us. That was an important first step in building the bond of trust I now share with the large group of Christian leaders—black, white, and brown—who make up President Trump's religious advisory board.

A DIFFERENT APPROACH

His approach was different, and it was dramatically successful. What the world discovered after the 2016 election was that Christian voters provided more than one-third of all the votes cast for Donald Trump. Although he received barely 8 percent of the black vote, subsequent polling indicated that large numbers of African Americans stayed home. Democrats have always taken our votes for granted, but conservative blacks had serious concerns about the motives, morals, and tactics of the Clintons.

Conservatives and dedicated Christians in our community couldn't bring themselves to vote for Hillary Clinton, so they stayed home. They weren't inclined to vote for the Republican candidate either, but by staying home, they denied Clinton the votes the Democrats expected from the swing states of Florida, Pennsylvania, Michigan, and Wisconsin. That proved to be Trump's big advantage.

For the most part, our communities believe in traditional marriage and reject the central platform issues of the Democratic Party.

For the most part, African American, Hispanic, and Asian communities believe in traditional marriage. They don't support same-sex marriage, and they reject the central platform issues of the Democratic Party, such as unrestricted abortion from conception to birth. Black Christians have a strong work ethic and believe in traditional moral values, which are key policy issues of the Republicans. Democrats, on the other hand, reject all those things. They have relied on identity politics for so long they've failed to recognize the growing discontent of African American voters and they've lost touch with the core values of these minority communities. The Trump campaign took our concerns seriously, and I believe that made all the difference.

Trump enjoyed the support of more than 80 percent of born-again Christians while Clinton received just 16 percent, which happened to be the lowest number ever recorded for a Democratic presidential candidate. Throughout the campaign, Trump reached out to Christian leaders in black and Hispanic communities. He actively sought our advice and asked for our support.

While no one would have called him a born-again believer at that time, he nevertheless spoke openly about his faith. He had grown up in a Presbyterian home, he said, and his Scottish mother instilled in him a love for God and the Bible. He promised to be a defender of the faith, and at a time like this, when Christian persecution is a growing threat around the world, that was enough to bring millions of Christian conservatives to the polls.

The politics of race has been a defining characteristic of Democratic politics for generations. A number of outspoken black leaders have exploited this practice to their own advantage, but many African Americans, Hispanics, Asians, and other minorities who have supported the Democrats with little to show for their faithfulness decided it was time to take a different approach. During the winter of 2019, every news channel was discussing how critical the black and Hispanic votes were for the Democratic Party. In fact, Joe Biden secured the Democratic presidential nomination by appealing to the minority voting bloc. Bernie Sanders was unable to convince these folks that he understood the minority dilemma despite his promise to give a great deal of free stuff.

If just 15 to 20 percent of minority voters leave the Democratic *big tent*, they will create a power shift that will attract the brightest minds of both parties to begin to compete for creative solutions to minority concerns—not just left versus right debates on issues of education, wealth creation, and minority entrepreneurship, but real problem solving, real recalibration, and real strategic thinking that aligns with Christian values to shine a light on a new path.

REGAINING OUR BEARINGS

I believe most Americans, regardless of race or economic status, want essentially the same things. We want to live in clean, safe neighborhoods; we want good jobs and a chance to make a decent living; and we want to feed our families, educate our children, and worship according to our core beliefs and cultural traditions. The approach that has driven minorities and inner-city families into the waiting arms of the Democratic Party for so many years was divisive and antagonistic. The rhetoric that teaches people to distrust their neighbors and believe that only government can solve their problems is self-serving, dishonest, and destructive.

As an evangelical leader and pastor of a large, predominately black congregation that includes members from over twenty-five nations, I have learned to love and serve members of this new coalition that I have been describing. I have also had the privilege of working closely with Donald Trump since before his election, and I am acutely aware that our president is not a racist. Many in my congregation believe he sincerely cares for the success and well-being of all American families. At the heart of his "make American great again" campaign theme is a desire to restore trust and mutual respect among the people of this country and overcome the social, economic, and political conditions that have robbed the nation of its peace and solidarity. Donald Trump knows that America will never be great again until we are truly the *United* States of America.

Even though I am also convinced that 2016 was a glimpse of what's ahead, the minority vote will determine the outcome of the 2020 election, and possibly many more to come. We should not forget that President Trump actually lost the popular vote in 2016 by a slim margin, while miraculously winning the Electoral College with 304 votes to Clinton's 227. Analysts on both sides of the political divide have said that a shift of only 5 to 7 percent of the newly empowered minority vote could determine the outcome of the next election. I am convinced the percentage will be much higher in 2020, but the key to building a strong minority coalition is the moral foundation that comes from our Christian faith and shared values.

Education, information, and mobilization are the keys to building bridges between our fractured communities.

Education, information, and mobilization are the keys to building bridges between our fractured communities. This means shifting our focus from the personalities of political candidates to the substance of their policies. The impeachment proceedings brought against President Trump in 2019 only served to polarize a dangerously divided United States.

Trying to unseat a duly elected president in that way, it seems to me, is the rankest form of partisanship. There is nothing in our constitution that allows an impeachment simply because the losing party feels embarrassed or humiliated. To deal with the issues that brought the nation to this point, we will need a reliable alternative based on time-honored biblical values, and that's the reason for this book and for all the work I am now doing.

When my dad decided to reroute the family trip to Norfolk, it was the only wise decision. Turning back would have disappointed everyone. Although the trip was longer and more arduous, he moved courageously ahead. After he got reoriented, he created a new route. A new challenge appeared on the horizon: would he blindly follow the new course in the evening darkness? Thankfully, he followed his new maps and local residents instead of his feelings.

CHAPTER 4

FOLLOWING NEW DIRECTIONS; UNDERSTANDING NEW GOVERNMENT AND YOUNGER VOTERS

In the last chapter, I described the process of rerouting my family's annual vacation. The annual drive to Norfolk could have been prolonged and made much easier by simply checking into a hotel and adding an additional twelve hours or more to the trip. We could have forgotten about my parents' urgency to get back home to enjoy *mommy and daddy time*. We could have simply overrun our precisely calculated budget. We would have had to pay for an additional night at a hotel and more meals. Maybe most significantly, Dad would have had to use another one or two of his precious days off. I think he wisely decided to press on. He embraced the new directions and braved the darkness of evening in what we thought was hostile Southern terrain.

Dad pressed past our family's concerns by simply trusting the directions. Minorities must decide that in the years ahead, we can trust our Declaration of Independence and our Constitution. Many minorities believe that their voice doesn't count, so they don't register to vote on the level they should. This chapter encourages *all* Christians of every ethnicity to engage in our political process—*following new directions*, as the chapter title suggests.

To grasp the need for civic engagement requires an understanding of the basic differences between three leading forms of government: monarchy, oligarchy, and representative democracy.

Simply put, monarchy is rule by a king or other key leaders. Overreach by the British sparked the Revolutionary War in America. The thirteen colonies that launched our fledgling nation chafed under restrictions imposed by the king. That sparked rebellions like the Boston Tea Party of 1773, which marked the culmination of long-simmering protests against English taxes and regulations. Colonists objected to duties being imposed without residents having a say in them.

Oligarchy is also a form of rule by the few. Under this system, people who are well-heeled, well-connected, or have special interests—be they political, religious, educational, or military—exert influence over government. In recent years, the U.S. has imposed sanctions on Russian oligarchs and their companies for supporting their government's nefarious activities, such as Russia's 2014 invasion of Ukraine, interference in other nations' elections, and the use of chemical weapons.

While some critics have accused the U.S. of having turned into an oligarchy, if that were true, Donald Trump could never have been elected president in 2016, since so many moneyed interests opposed him. In a representative democracy, people still have the right to elect the president and other representatives who make decisions governing their country.

It's important to understand that the U.S. is not a *direct* democracy but a democratic republic. *We the people* don't make the laws by majority vote. In a republic, people choose those who will ultimately make decisions regarding taxes, government policies, and public institutions. Understanding this distinction is a key to understanding why grassroots citizen action is vital to our nation's welfare. We the people can still elect our leaders and express our views when it comes to determining our future. To disregard this right is to scorn our birthright and allow others to rule our lives.

To disregard our right to elect our leaders and express our views is to scorn our birthright and allow others to rule our lives.

The LGBTQ lobby and others have successfully changed public policy by using constitutional rights to affect the law. Gay activists used the same legal strategies followed during the civil rights era to bring change and address what they saw as injustice and oppression. Understanding the tools they used matters more than what you think about a particular cause.

The LGBTQ strategy followed the one outlined in *Root and Branch: Charles Hamilton Houston, Thurgood Marshall, and the Struggle to End Segregation.* [21] This landmark book by attorney Rawn James Jr., a former assistant attorney general for the District of Columbia, traces the groundbreaking work by the Harvard-educated Houston, a Howard University law professor, and his student—a future Supreme Court justice. The pair created the legal strategy used to attack segregation, a cultural practice contradicting the nation's founding ideal that all men are created equal. Their long-term fight culminated in the 1954 ruling *Brown v. Board of Education*. Although it took years of protest and civil disobedience after this historic Supreme Court ruling to finally end segregation, it is now outlawed in practice as well as theory.

Using this approach, which secured equality and biblical justice for African Americans, LGBTQ voices pressed their case in the nation's courts and were successful with the 2015 *Obergefell v. Hodges* decision that legalized same-sex marriage. Not content to stop there, gay activists continue to press their case, lobbying for legislation such as the Equality Act—passed by the U.S. House of Representatives in May 2019—which would prohibit discrimination based on factors such as sexual orientation and gender identity. The bill remains in the Senate, but the far-reaching impact of this proposed law can already be seen. Even without it, transgender men have secured the right to compete in women's sports in high school and college, where biological males' genetic makeup gives them an obvious advantage that many female athletes decry as unfair.

SPIRITUAL AWAKENING

This kind of change underscores Christians' need to wake up and utilize our freedom of speech as we pursue grassroots action. While a host of ultra-liberal and leftist groups willingly press their case in the public square, too many Christians sit idly by, too intimidated to speak up, too busy to vote, or too apathetic to care about what is happening around them.

We need a religious awakening, a revival of personal holiness and adherence to biblical truth.

When I say we need a religious awakening in the U.S., I don't mean churches should rule the government. I'm talking about the need for a revival of personal holiness and adherence to biblical truth, which isn't dictated by law but expressed by the heart. Too many church members think we can outlaw all kinds of drugs and deviant personal behavior, but laws won't change people. What's required is a heart transformation, something only God can do.

With such an awakening, we would see:

+ *Unity* among the different ethnicities who worship in churches across our land, less bickering within churches, and less stone-throwing between different groups and denominations.

+ *Increased vitality* in our economy, as integrity in personal dealings affects commerce and society as a whole.

+ *Decreased crime rates.* During the Second Great Awakening in the 1800s, such a sense of God prevailed that taverns and bars closed, resulting in less drunkenness and violence. When Charles Finney, the father of modern revivalism, preached in Rochester, New York, in 1830–31, it so stirred the city that people closed down the taverns and turned the only theater into a livery stable and the only circus into a soap and candle factory. These are practical signs of spiritual awakening.

In addition to a more law-abiding citizenry, we would see more followers of Christ active and involved in their communities—people who care about their fellow human beings, not seeking to rule over others but to serve them. They would become prayer warriors as well as politically active believers who research issues, vote, and press their case with elected representatives.

Today, some Christians are mildly engaged in the political arena, but not enough follow through. In major elections, only 50 percent of Christians are registered to vote and only half of them turn out. Thus, just 25 percent of the church makes its will known concerning the day's vital issues. It helps that prayer warriors are concerned about abortion and other cultural flaws, but imagine the impact if they got up off their knees and went to their precinct on Election Day—and inspired others to do the same.

PRESSING THE CASE

The need to transform beliefs about moral and social issues often calls for taking a stand in the political arena. This reality has motivated numerous ministries, organizations, and citizen groups to move toward tangible action.

A prime example is the Family Research Council (FRC), which started in 1981 as an outgrowth of Dr. James Dobson's Focus on the Family (FOF). When Dobson launched FOF in 1977, he wanted to strengthen families weakened by divorce, moral decay, and powerful special interest groups. Dobson finally took this cause to Washington, DC.

Although the two groups later separated, FRC became an influential conservative voice. The council's former president, Gary Bauer, briefly ran for the Republican nomination for president in 2000. Today, FRC President Tony Perkins speaks out about family, social, and moral issues through the council's website, Facebook, Twitter, and other electronic means. He makes numerous appearances on TV networks and in other media forums.

Other FRC staff weigh in on pro-life issues such as abortion, euthanasia, stem cell research, women's health, and protections for the right of conscience so that pro-life doctors cannot be forced to perform an abortion. The council addresses family, parental, and sexuality concerns as well, including the need to teach abstinence and fight pornography.

While not directly connected to FRC, more than three dozen statewide Family Policy Councils carry on the work of helping to shape debate and influence policy on a local and statewide level.

Inaccurate stereotyping led the Southern Poverty Law Center to label the Family Research Council an "anti-gay hate group."

Not surprisingly, this has inspired criticism and inaccurate stereotyping, such as the Southern Poverty Law Center (SPLC) labeling FRC an "anti-gay hate group." In 2012, a gunman showed up at FRC's headquarters, citing the SPLC's designation as his motivation. Perkins later said:

The SPLC's reckless labeling has led to devastating consequences. Because of its "hate group" labeling, a deadly terrorist had a guidemap to FRC and other organizations. Our team is still dealing with the fallout of the attack, that was intended to have a chilling effect on organizations that are simply fighting for their values. [22]

Another leading think tank, the Heritage Foundation, was organized in 1973 to promote free enterprise, limited government, individual freedom, and traditional American values. It first took a leading role in the conservative movement during Ronald Reagan's presidency. In 2017, Kay Coles James—director of the U.S. Office of Personnel Management under President George W. Bush—became the foundation's first African American president.

Naturally, this organization has also prompted bitter criticism from liberal voices. That hasn't dimmed its effectiveness: in early 2020, a University of Pennsylvania study ranked it the leading think tank for impact on public policy for the third consecutive year.

As you can see, political advocacy stirs up controversy. The hubbub can scare away Christians who don't want to be seen as hate mongers or irrational, ignorant extremists. While there are radical elements in any movement, believers shouldn't allow this to prevent them from engaging in the discussion. To remain silent for fear of being stereotyped or aiding those on the fringes only dims our cause and encourages the opposition.

COLOR WITH CLOUT

The aforementioned conservative organizations are predominantly white, but there are also groups of color that have influenced public policy. Few are better known than the NAACP, founded in 1909 as the National Association for the Advancement of Colored People, the latter a term that has passed into disuse in the American lexicon.

The organization played a crucial role during the civil rights era, first challenging segregation in Maryland schools. The case led to the formation of the NAACP's Legal Defense Fund, which supported the desegregation efforts that led to the *Brown v. Board of Education* decision. Eighteen months later, the NAACP helped to organize the year-long bus boycott in Montgomery, Alabama. This successful protest planted the seeds for lunch counter sit-ins and other forms of civil disobedience that followed.

Over the years, the NAACP has been a key voice in African Americans' lives through such action as fighting to outlaw lynching, challenging the denial of voting rights, and opposing discrimination in employment. While I don't agree with some of its stances, such as its support of same-sex marriage, the NAACP has nevertheless been a major presence that has left an indelible imprint on American society.

Founded the year after the NAACP, the National Urban League has been another prominent voice in the battle for civil rights and equal opportunity in employment, housing, and education. Though based in New York, it maintains a Washington bureau to serve as its research and policy arm, including advocacy before Congress and the executive branch.

An organizational member of the forty-five-year-old Coalition to Stop Gun Violence, more recently the Urban League has sought to enhance the voice of black Americans through media productions, such as *The State of Black America Town Hall*, which aired on TV One in 2017 and 2018, and a weekly iTunes podcast, *For the Movement*, which reviews policy, social, and civil rights issues.

The grassroots movement Black Lives Matter (BLM) sprang up in 2013 after George Zimmerman was acquitted in the shooting of Trayvon Martin in Florida. Originally a

Facebook group, BLM has called attention to abuses of power. Their first in-person protest came after the shooting of Michael Brown in Ferguson, Missouri, in 2014. They have spotlighted travesties such as the 2014 choking death of Eric Garner by a New York City police officer, the 2016 police shooting of Minnesota motorist Philando Castile after he simply reached for his wallet, and the 2018 shooting of Markeis McGlockton, an unarmed Florida man, in a dispute with another man over a parking space.

ADDRESSING A NEED FOR AWARENESS

Without the public awareness sparked by BLM, I don't know if the gunman behind that 2018 shooting would have later been convicted of manslaughter, or if the police officer who shot the motorist reaching for his wallet would have been charged with murder. Who's to say?

However, BLM comes with a caveat: liberal underpinnings. Two of the three female founders are gay, and another organizer identifies as transgender. Not surprisingly, it bills itself as a queer-affirming network and an anti-nuclear-family voice—things a majority of African Americans do not embrace.

While Black Lives Matter has brought awareness to important issues, it bills itself as a queer-affirming network and an anti-nuclear-family voice.

That's why I believe we need more black conservative organizations, such as Black Voices for Trump. The group's advisory board includes such figures as former presidential hopeful Herman Cain and Pastor Darrell Scott. The nature of such a group among people who largely vote Democratic and are largely anti-Trump is so unusual that the opening of a field office in Milwaukee in March 2020 drew coverage from National Public Radio. [23]

Other voices are also emerging, such as David Harris Jr., author of *Why I Couldn't Stay Silent*, a book about his personal political awakening. [24] The California businessman appeared at the November 2018 Young Black Leadership Summit and continues to reach a social media audience estimated at 1.4 million.

In Harris's eyes, the leading reason to oppose Democrats' lies is the party's championing of abortion. From an early age, Harris, who was raised in a Christian home, placed a high value on unborn babies, believing they deserve the same care, protection, and nurturing as the women carrying them. Saying abortion has "decimated" the black community, Harris believes too many African Americans fail to recognize the truth of what is happening.

"When I began to look at how Barack Obama had voted, I realized he had voted for partial birth abortion—which is literally dismembering babies in the womb," Harris says. "Then I discovered that he also voted against a bill that would have provided medical treatment to babies that survived abortion. So I didn't care what color he was at that point. He was not going to get my vote."

Harris said his mother told him to pay attention to how politicians vote, not what they say. Thus, he says, he couldn't vote for Democrats because their platform includes support for abortion.

Still, Harris didn't become active until after the third debate between Hillary Clinton and Donald Trump. Aside from the abortion issue, he finds many things to like about the president, such as providing $255 million in funding for historically black colleges and universities. Harris says Trump is the one who implemented prison reform, lowered unemployment dramatically, and did a better job dealing with the coronavirus than President Obama did with swine flu in 2009.

"I would so much rather have the president that has been so effective on so many fronts ... handling this virus than any other Democrat out there," Harris says. "I would be scared to think of what a Bernie Sanders or Joe Biden would do."

VOTER ENGAGEMENT

While some African American evangelical Christians continue to vote for Democratic candidates, white evangelicals remain one of the GOP's most reliable voting blocs. A 2016 CNN exit poll found that 57 percent of white voters supported Trump in the 2016 presidential election. But among white evangelical Christians, the support was even higher, with 80 percent voting for Trump and only 16 percent supporting Clinton. [25]

Even two years later, during the midterm elections, when Democratic gains in the House were seen by many as a referendum on Trump's administration, some 75 percent of white evangelical Christians supported Republican House candidates, according to National Election Pool (NEP) exit poll data. That figure was consistent with the 78 percent and 77 percent of white evangelicals who supported Republicans in the 2014 and 2010 midterms, respectively. [26]

Election turnout has long been key to the strength of the white evangelical voting bloc. Although white evangelicals comprise 17 percent of the population, they have made up roughly 25 percent of voters in the last three election cycles. [27] While that has always been good news for Republicans, younger and minority evangelicals are not following the same voting trends, with higher percentages of those groups supporting Democratic candidates.

According to a study conducted by the Billy Graham Center Institute at Wheaton College and LifeWay Research, 52 percent of self-identified evangelicals between the ages of eighteen and thirty-four and 47 percent of those thirty-five to forty-nine voted for Hillary Clinton, the Democratic presidential nominee in 2016. [28] Compare that with the 67 percent of self-identified evangelicals sixty-five and older who voted for Trump.

The same survey found that 86 percent of African Americans who held evangelical beliefs and 85 percent of those who self-identified as evangelicals voted for Hillary Clinton. The Pew Research Center reported that 6 percent of African American voters supported Trump. And according to AP VoteCast, roughly 80 percent of black evangelicals who voted during the 2018 midterms said they disapproved of President Trump's performance. [29]

Many black people are quietly leaving the Democratic Party— mostly, as one woman observes, "because of the Tyranny of the Alphabet People."

Yet a November 2019 Emerson poll gave Trump a 34.5 percent approval rating among African American voters, and according to a January 2020 Gallup poll, there was a 14 percent increase in satisfaction over race relations among Americans. [30]

It is a trend one African American woman observed in a blog posted on the American Conservative website, where she noted that she had encountered many black people "over the past few years who do not hate Trump, are quietly divesting from the Democratic Party—mostly because of the Tyranny of the Alphabet People—and are closet fans of people like Thomas Sowell, Candace Owens and Sheriff David Clarke." [31] African Americans who vote for Republicans "are, indisputably, a distinct minority," she said, adding:

> I highly doubt that more than 10% of black voters will pull the lever for Donald Trump in 2020. What is worth noting, however, and is often ignored, is that a number of black voters are simply going to sit the thing out. They're not going to vote for Trump, but they are also not going to vote for the agenda of people who think that "trans is the new black." [32]

Much the same can likely be said of politically conservative evangelicals within other minority groups. In her 2018 book *Immigrants, Evangelicals, and Politics in an Era of Demographic Change*, Janelle S. Wong reported that while more than one in seven evangelicals in the U.S. is Asian American or Hispanic, less than 40 percent of Asian American voters and less than 30 percent of Latino evangelicals said they voted for Trump in 2016. [33] It is clear that while there is agreement on some traditionally conservative issues such as abortion, nonwhite evangelical voters have distinct political priorities and realities.

Wong noted that together, Asian Americans, Hispanics, and African Americans make up nearly one-third of evangelicals overall [34] but their views tend to be "significantly less conservative than those of their white counterparts. Black, Asian American, and Latino evangelicals are much more likely to support policies such as expanded immigration rights, increased taxation of the wealthy, and government interventions to slow climate change." Wong argues that non-white evangelicals' experiences as members of racial or ethnic minority groups often lead them to adopt more progressive political views than their white counterparts. [35]

Non-white evangelicals' experiences as members of racial or ethnic minority groups often lead them to adopt progressive political views.

Minority voter turnout has seen gains, with Hispanics making up 9.2 percent of voters in 2016, up from 8.4 percent in 2012. Asian Americans also saw growth, increasing from 2.8 percent of all voters to 3.6 percent in 2016. Yet while white voter turnout held steady at 73.3 percent, African Americans made up 11.9 percent of voters in 2016, down from 12.9 percent in 2012. [36]

Those numbers, however, don't tell the whole story. Pew reported that there were a record 12.7 million Hispanic voters in 2016, up from 11.2 million in 2012. Yet 14 million Hispanics who were eligible to vote did not cast a ballot, making the number of nonvoters higher than the number of voters. Perhaps because of this trend, the voter turnout rate among Asian Americans surpassed that of Hispanic voters for the first time since 1996, increasing from 46.9 percent in 2012 to 49.3 percent in 2016. Still, the number of Asian American voters remains smaller at 5 million in 2016 compared to 3.8 million in 2012. [37]

Midterm election turnout is typically lower than the general election, and that proved true in 2018. Yet voter turnout improved in 2018, with 53.4 percent of eligible voters casting their ballots that year, up from 41.9 percent in 2014. The largest increase was among those between the ages of eighteen and twenty-nine, a group that went from 20 percent turnout in 2014 to 36 percent in 2018. The turnout of both African American and Hispanic voters increased by 11 percent over 2014. And Asian American voter turnout increased from 26.9 percent to 40.2 percent in 2014. [38]

Still, a large percentage of minority voters tend to stay home, some because of their immigration status, but many others simply because they aren't registered to vote or don't think their vote will matter.

In some states, minority evangelicals could decide the election, yet many believe their groups are being overlooked by both major political parties.

In some states, minority evangelicals could decide the election, yet many believe their groups are being overlooked by both Democrats and Republicans. They say the parties either presume they already have the group's vote, as is often the case with African American evangelical voters, or they don't know how to court a group with so much internal diversity, as is the case with Hispanic voters. For instance, in Florida, Cuban American voters have long leaned Republican, while those with a Puerto Rican heritage lean Democratic. Florida's population of the latter grew in 2017 when many moved to the state to escape the devastation caused by Hurricane Maria.

"Most Latinos will tend to be socially conservative on issues like abortion and same-sex marriage but will tend to be social liberals on issues like education and immigration, so we've tended to be divided on how we spread the vote," Juan Martínez told *Christianity Today*. "Those of us who have voted have struggled with this for years because the Democrat/Republican way that this is broken out doesn't fit us well." [39]

We must build bridges across racial and ethnic lines to create a coalition that seeks righteousness and justice in the political sphere.

Minority evangelical communities are growing, and their political influence is still gaining traction. What would happen if the church were to build bridges across racial and ethnic lines to create a coalition that sought righteousness and justice in the political sphere? I, for one, don't think it's too much to ask.

CHALLENGES REMAIN

While there are encouraging signs, conservatives face formidable challenges, too, none stronger than the need to form new voter coalitions. This is especially true among millennials and Gen Xers, since younger adults appear to be moving in a liberal direction. Fifty-nine percent of millennials are registered Democrats and Americans under the age of thirty voted for the party's candidates by a 35-point margin in the 2018 mid-term elections.

A pair of 2019 Pew Research Center surveys showed that among teens and young adults, only three in ten approve of how Trump is handling his job as president. A mirror image of 70 percent thought government should do more to solve problems, rather than doing too many things better left to businesses and individuals.

Commenting on the seeming dichotomy between young and old, longtime Republican Kori Schake—who served as an advisor to the 2008 John McCain presidential campaign—said in a 2019 article for *The Atlantic* that Republicans are failing to win the minds and hearts of young voters. She wrote:

Americans under the age of 30 had as their formative experiences the era of terrorism, the mistakes of wars in Iraq and Afghanistan, and the 2008 financial crisis, all of which they associate with the Republican Party.

And they revile the depredations of Trump's behavior and procedural contortions by Senate Republicans to partisan purposes (like the refusal to vote on the Supreme Court nominee Merrick Garland). What we as a conservative movement look like to young Americans is old, white, male, bigoted, and unprincipled—people who bray loudly at others breaking the rules but excuse ourselves doing so. [40]

Obviously, Black Voices for Trump and Donald Harris Jr. contradict that kind of image, but we still have a long way to go in counteracting it. It's time to follow a new road map—full speed ahead.

ENGAGING IN GOVERNMENT

If Christians want to truly engage in our representative government we must do three things:

1. We must articulate our desires. That's why I'm suggesting this Manifesto or declaration.

2. We must create or invent new language that expresses our views in a winsome way. In the future, liberal versus conservative descriptions will have to be reframed to adopt a language that describes righteousness and justice. (More on this in chapter nine.)

3. We must decide to *travel together*. As we become one engaged voice, we will have influence, spiritual power, cultural consequence, and impact.

After that last car trip forced my normally jovial father to deal with construction detours and more time on the road, my parents had to decide whether we would travel together. Ultimately, they decided to send me and Eric to Norfolk by train. My parents stayed home and relaxed while my brother and I received the benefits of the family connection. My parents loved the break … but something was missing. And it was intimidating for two preteen boys to change trains. As the oldest, the sense of responsibility I felt was almost overwhelming. I loved Norfolk but hated the train.

Thankfully, our family decided to travel together once again the following year.

As we apply the family vacation analogy to our Christian engagement journey, we must travel together these first few years for many reasons. In the next chapter, we will discuss the costs and benefits of traveling together. Some believe that we're going to need racial or ethnic healing first, but I believe that healing can take place as we go. You may be surprised at how easy this united journey can be if we have the right mindset.

CHAPTER 5

TRAVELING TOGETHER TOWARD A NEW CONSENSUS

Eric recently reminded me that when we drove from Cincinnati, Ohio, to Norfolk, Virginia, and back, we passed through regions with differing degrees of acceptance of our blackness. In some areas, there were sit-down restaurants that would not serve us. Sometimes, we didn't even feel safe enough to stop and use the restrooms. Therefore, Dad would often start our trip so early in the morning that we had been driving for hours when the sun finally came up. Leaving at four o'clock in the morning ensured that we would pass through intimidating regions while the sun was still high.

During the years we made this pilgrimage, my brother only remembers one sit-down breakfast we had together as a family. He says we were served by a white waitress in a very clean restaurant.

For our return trip, Big Mama would frequently pack a picnic basket filled with fried chicken, rolls, snacks, and assorted goodies, so we didn't have to stop for food. In his professional life, my father had a great job, as the doors were opened for blacks to climb the ladders of public success. But in private and personal ways, we still felt the exclusion and persecution that came from the Jim Crow era of American history. After reviewing public assimilation for blacks and other minorities, we will explore how the church can be more accepting of minorities. I hope you enjoy the ride.

In the following discussion, drawn in part from my book, *The Truth in Black and White*, [41] I want to take these issues a step further by focusing on how social conditions are affecting the pursuit of equal status and opportunities for minorities in our nation. America continues to espouse a concept of meritocracy, in which our society is essentially colorblind and the best person gets the job or opportunity. While we are making real progress, many minority people and poor whites still feel that they are locked out of the places of highest power. They want an access card, or they want to figure out how to pay their dues at the *good old boys' club*.

I live in the metro area of Washington, DC, where a new assimilation of whites and upwardly mobile, middle-class blacks seems to be taking place. But this time, it is not happening through noisy confrontation and debate, but as a natural consequence of people becoming acquainted with each other through their schools, workplaces, and churches.

What the Great Society social engineers tried to accomplish through busing and forced integration was a failure.

What the Great Society social engineers tried to accomplish through busing and other kinds of forced integration was, for the most part, a failure. President Lyndon B. Johnson believed he could create the Great Society by fiat, and he used a Democrat-controlled Congress and the federal bureaucracy to force through measures that would never have passed muster at the ballot box. There was no opportunity to evaluate what was working and what wasn't, so the American people simply said no.

This is an important teaching point. One of the major problems with politics is that candidates get elected or receive funding by making big promises, not by saying they want to keep the status quo or make a few minor improvements. They campaign on big dreams and offer all kinds of visionary programs, and when they get to Washington, they create legislative monstrosities that cost billions of taxpayer dollars and accomplish very little—or make things worse.

This is part of what went wrong with the mandates of the civil rights era. Government's top-down solutions to problems in education, welfare, affirmative action, and poverty failed to deliver the goods. Yes, we need some kind of response to address the damage done by previous generations, but it must come naturally through human interaction, not by judicial mandate or presidential executive orders.

On the other hand, there is a tendency for the white middle class to say, "We don't need to do anything. You people just need to lift yourself up by your bootstraps." But, honestly, that is not enough. To say, "You've got a problem—deal with it!" doesn't work, and it certainly isn't Christian. If there is one thing we have learned from liberals, it is that government cannot simply demand moral behavior. The liberals' way has not worked, but the conservatives' only response has been complaints.

There aren't many working models where conservatives have come forward with a better idea of how to improve the lives of minorities. It's as if they're saying, "You're on your own now, so fix it. And don't blame me if you fail!" There is something unsettling about this attitude for most African Americans. I would like to think that the leaders of the evangelical movement are beginning to figure that out.

On the other hand, many blacks have not taken ownership of a negative generational transfer. One of the things we have learned from the violence in places like Ferguson, Missouri, and Jena, Louisiana, is that the younger generation is still harboring the anger of the previous generation. We wonder why their mothers didn't tell these kids, "Look, violence is not the answer. You've got to live together!" And yet that takes us back to the issue of education and preparation for life in today's high-tech, global society. Too many people in our neighborhoods don't have a grasp of their own history, the journey our people have made, or even the most basic history of the U.S.

Too many people don't have a grasp of their own history, the journey our people have made, or even the most basic history of the U.S.

Our young people need to be challenged to think about our past. What got our people out of slavery? Was it because our ancestors had the military might to overthrow the Confederate Army? Of course not. It was because white Christians, moved by the Holy Spirit, created the abolitionist movement. These men and women were intermediaries for blacks before, during, and after the Civil War. It is true that many African Americans served in the military—the movie *Glory* provides a great example of the courage they exhibited [42] —but there would never have been an opportunity for a *Glory* regiment if there had not been benevolent whites who fought to end slavery.

Time and time again, I have found that it has taken a multiracial alliance to break the stronghold of systemic social injustice. Did you know that the NAACP was founded by a majority white leadership group in early 1910? W. E. B. Du Bois was the lone black member of this historic coalition and served as director of publicity and research. The other original officers were:

- National president, Moorfield Storey, a white man from Boston
- Chairman of the executive committee, William English Walling, who came from a wealthy family in Kentucky
- Treasurer, John E. Milholland, a Lincoln Republican and Presbyterian from New York City
- Disbursing treasurer, Oswald Garrison Villard, editor of the *New York Evening Post*
- Executive secretary, Frances Blascoer, a white woman

The NAACP's mission was "to promote equality of rights and eradicate caste or race prejudice among the citizens of the United States; to advance the interest of colored citizens; to secure for them impartial suffrage; and to increase their opportunities for securing justice in the courts, education for the children, employment according to their ability and complete equality before law." The NAACP pursued this mission through a variety of tactics, including legal action, lobbying, peaceful protest, and publicity.

KNOWING HOW TO ADAPT

When I was growing up, I would sometimes hear people say, "Young man, you're a credit to your race," or something along those lines. Such statements weren't offensive to me then, but they would annoy or even outrage most blacks today. Comments like that imply that African Americans have to work harder to prove themselves. Whether we like it or not, it's true. We *do* have to work harder to be noticed. But sometimes, working a little harder can lead to some big rewards.

Statements like, "Young man, you're a credit to your race" would annoy or even outrage most blacks today.

The private high school I attended gave me a great education, but I also learned some undesirable behaviors from kids in my neighborhood. In school, I learned the King's English. On the weekends, I started hanging around with a group of kids who thought it was cool to use ghetto talk and all kinds of slang. It wasn't long before my mother put a stop to that. As an elementary school teacher, she never let me use slang at home. The dinner table was almost sacred ground for language. Mom believed that education was the way to a better life, and she wanted her children to speak properly. Many immigrant families who come here from other countries and other ethnic traditions also strive to mainstream themselves linguistically.

My parents would say, "Harry, people are going to judge you by how you talk, so at least in this house, we don't want you using that slang." And I understood that. Regardless of what we believe about this issue, anyone coming to this country cannot expect to be successful or share in the general prosperity of our nation unless they become fluent in standard American English. That doesn't mean they have to lose their culture or their heritage, but if they want to get ahead, they have to learn the English language and the American culture.

I am reminded of another experience I had not long ago at an event with a lot of young people. An attractive black woman in her early thirties told me that she, too, had a mother who insisted that she speak correctly. This young woman was very articulate and clear in the way she spoke. With her hair braids and her funky outfit, she looked like a typical *sister from the hood*, but she had a wonderful gift for language. At one point, she said, "I speak two languages. I can speak Ebonics when I need to, or I can speak textbook English. That's the heritage I was given." I was glad to hear that she was not only proud of her heritage, but also able to succeed in the broader culture.

UNEQUAL OPPORTUNITY

One of the most misunderstood issues that has been hotly debated for more than fifty years now is *affirmative action*. The term was first used in 1961 during the administration of John Kennedy, when the president authorized preferential hiring of minorities under Executive Order 10925. Subsequently, both public and private organizations began talking about establishing *quotas* and *set-asides*, referring to the process of recruiting and hiring minority applicants. Kennedy's executive order was revolutionary in scope, but the original idea was very simple.

The directive specified that federal contractors should take positive steps to ensure that all Americans would have equal access to jobs and appointments "without regard to race, creed, color, or national origin." [43] Although such issues had been addressed by the administrations of both Franklin Roosevelt and Harry Truman years earlier, this was the first time the government actually set out to change and monitor hiring practices based on race.

Today, six decades later, affirmative action is being used in everything from awarding government contracts to the hiring of corporate executives and public school teachers. Whites, Asian Americans, and others have challenged the policy repeatedly on the grounds that they are not being allowed to compete for jobs on the basis of merit. They claim to be victims of *reverse discrimination*.

Affirmative action is still a hot-button issue, and it's another area that has led to antagonism between the races. But the origins of the affirmative action debate actually precede the Kennedy administration. Like the busing issue of the 1960s, it can be traced back to the 1954 Supreme Court decision *Brown v. Board of Education*, which was argued on the basis of the Equal Protection Clause of the Fourteenth Amendment to the Constitution. This clause holds that no state shall "deny to any person within its jurisdiction the equal protection of the laws."

Linda Brown was a third-grade black child who had been denied admission to an all-white school. In a unanimous opinion written by Chief Justice Earl Warren, the court said, "Separate education facilities are inherently unequal." Segregating children solely on the basis of race, Warren said, "generates a feeling of inferiority as to their status in the community that may affect their hearts and minds in a way unlikely ever to be undone."

Interpretations of that ruling were later included in the Civil Rights Act of 1964 and Executive Order 11246, issued by President Johnson, which specifically mandated affirmative action hiring and promotion of minority faculty members at Howard University, one of America's premier historically black colleges. However, delays in implementing these new policies caused later administrations to specify that goals and timetables should be established to ensure compliance.

We need to examine the ethical and legal consequences of continuing affirmative action nearly sixty years after the Civil Rights Act of 1964.

Over the years, there have been attempts to enforce quotas and proportional representation of minorities, but today, the groups most affected by these rulings have questioned the ethical and legal consequences of continuing affirmative action nearly sixty years after the Civil Rights Act of 1964, and more than 157 years after the Emancipation Proclamation.

When Martin Luther King Jr. challenged institutional racism in the 1950s and 1960s, he began by organizing voter registration drives throughout the South. He led rallies in his hometown of Albany, Georgia, in 1962, and then in Birmingham, Alabama, and Danville, Virginia, in 1963. He also organized the historic March on Washington in August 1963, where he spoke the oft-quoted, stirring words, "I have a dream that my four little children will one day live in a nation where they will not be judged by the color of their skin but by the content of their character."

King's idea of change wasn't based on force but on the power of persuasion and the Christian's obligation to *"honor one another"* (Romans 12:10). Those who felt that affirmative action created an unequal playing field pointed out that the new laws were not concerned about character, but only the color of a person's skin, and were thus fundamentally unfair. However, King and others pointed out that the majority of blacks in this country were living in substandard housing, working at substandard jobs, and enduring substandard treatment at the hands of the white majority—all unfair circumstances. Affirmative action and financial assistance for the poor were merely an attempt to restore the balance, they said. But none of these arguments would calm the storm of controversy that was rising in the land.

DEALING WITH RESENTMENT

Part of the polarization of society at that time came down to the fact that many felt that affirmative action was being forced on an unwilling population by government edict rather than reason or compassion on a human level. The main problem with the government's approach was the attempt to enforce not just equal opportunity but also equal results. Some people went so far as to imagine what would happen if that standard were applied in professional sports. In the end, the attempt to enforce equal results proved hurtful to the men and women for whom the affirmative action programs were meant to help, since they created a hostile work environment and increased the levels of mistrust between whites and blacks.

The attempt to enforce equal results created a hostile work environment and increased the levels of mistrust between whites and blacks.

Many of the problems of affirmative action in the workplace were repeated in schools and colleges where affirmative action admissions had been implemented. By placing minority students in academic settings for which they were unprepared, affirmative action enrollments guaranteed that many would fail. Until recently, only 40 percent of new freshman at the University of California were admitted on the basis of academic merit, with the majority admitted primarily on the basis of race. With minority children still experiencing scholastic achievement gaps in their primary and secondary school years, [44] what are their chances of success in college?

This is a sticky issue for me. I am sure that my admission to the famous Williams College, often rated as the top liberal arts college in the nation, was influenced by my championship sports background and my race. Later, in the late 1970s, I received a grant to attend Harvard Business School in order to earn my MBA.

Here's the dynamic: at the elite universities most likely to give preferential admission to minority students, the dropout rate of nonwhites is consistently higher than that of whites. Such things should concern us, not just because of the problems created by the government's heavy-handed meddling, but also because the Christian tradition offers a better way. Those who believe in the founding principles of this nation—"that all men are created equal, that they are endowed by their Creator with certain unalienable rights"—ought to understand the innate worth of all of God's people, who come from all races and national backgrounds. White society has been slow to accept this point of view, but policies that divide us on the basis of race, no matter how well-intentioned they may be, don't do much for "life, liberty, and the pursuit of happiness."

NAACP founder W. E. B. Du Bois received his Ph.D. from Harvard in 1895. Ten years later, he founded the Niagara Movement, a black civil rights organization dedicated to social and political change for African Americans. The author of the classic work *The Souls of Black Folk*, Du Bois lived to the ripe old age of ninety-five.

Du Bois was a member of what he and Christian intellectuals called the "talented tenth," their theory being that at least 10 percent of every race had the potential to become leaders. This concept came from Christian theologians and the American Baptist Home Mission Society, which was strongly supported by John D. Rockefeller.

But racial stereotypes and the sinful behavior of discrimination barred both the talented tenth and the "average" members of all minorities from many aspects of the American dream. Cruelty, terrorism, torture, lynching, and worse had become part of what many call America's original sin. For the nation to simply go forward without addressing those facts would have been unacceptable. What was our nation to do to cleanse itself from such inhumane treatment of blacks, Hispanics, Asians, and other immigrants? We probably should have developed two tracks: a secular, government track and a Christian church and family track.

Rather than resorting to legal sanctions alone, we as Christians need to remember that "God shows no partiality"—and neither should we.

Rather than resorting to legal sanctions alone, we still need to remember the words of the apostle Peter, who says in Acts, "*God shows no partiality. But in every nation whoever fears Him and works righteousness is accepted by Him*" (Acts 10:35 NKJV). This challenge is repeated countless times in Scripture, which tells us that we are all equal in the eyes of God and "*partiality,*" or prejudice, is forbidden. As Paul says, "*There is neither Jew nor Gentile, neither slave nor free, nor is there male and female, for you are all one in Christ Jesus*" (Galatians 3:28).

Furthermore, we are told that nothing can separate us from the love of God. Paul goes on to say, "*If you belong to Christ, then you are Abraham's seed, and heirs according to the promise*" (verse 29). In other words, we are commanded to live as equals even when race, customs, and history would seem to divide us. If we are truly children of God, social programs based on behaviorist theories of enforced equality can be dangerous and counterproductive, as has often been the case. But if we listen to the Word of God, there is a better way—the way of love. After all, "*God is love*" (1 John 4:8).

Sociologists can produce all kinds of economic and social data showing why affirmative action is a good idea. Furthermore, I do believe that *some* forms of affirmative action are still needed, such as giving black businesses an equal opportunity to compete for contracts or other ventures. In the end, however, it is not about equal opportunity; it's about our responsibility as Christians to live in accordance with what we say we believe. This is an area where the new black church and other minority churches can lead the way. The Bible does not allow any place for ending prejudice by force. Rather, it tells us the law of God is written on the heart. (See Jeremiah 31:33.)

TIME TO TAKE ACTION

During an interview on *The Tavis Smiley Show* on the BET network, I was asked to explain my view of what a new paradigm for black voters would look like. I told Smiley that my purpose in creating a moral agenda for black voters was to develop a set of public policy priorities that would go beyond the standard Democratic Party fare. I said, "This is something that black people care about. This is an area of common ground on which we can all agree and which we are committed to supporting through the political process."

Until now, I said, black voters have not been very good about going into the political process with an agenda. Most of the time, we just come up with complaints because we've trusted people who haven't been very good at delivering on their promises. Time and time again, we trust them to take our interests to heart, and then we're surprised when they let us down. The unfortunate result is that a lot of blacks don't vote—they stay home because they've given up. And there are still a great many black voters who just pull the Democratic lever because "we've always done it that way."

We've reached the point where words alone are not enough. Most of the liberal policies we have supported in the past do not work. But the good news is that, thanks to the momentum and energy coming from Trump's stunning victory in 2016, there is a new openness to the ideas of people in the black community. I believe Donald Trump is a big part of that because he refused to let liberal Democrats set the national agenda. He took on the Democrats in Congress and began to shed light on the dangers of the *deep state* and the corrupt permanent bureaucracy.

There is a new generation of voters coming along who are open to morally responsible conservative policies.

From the beginning, Trump has made a powerful appeal to minority voters who are serious about making a better life for themselves and their families. This means there is a new generation of voters coming along who are open to morally responsible conservative policies. It is making a difference, and we can see it happening. But the window of opportunity will not remain open for long if we fail to accept this challenge and if our elected officials fail to deliver on their promises.

An article by public policy analyst Stewart Lawrence in *The Federalist* makes this point very well. Lawrence says that Trump's outreach to African Americans has given him an opening that Republicans have not experienced in a very long time. He writes:

> Despite condemning Trump publicly as a bigot, Democrats are privately worried about this. They should be. Two recent and highly reputable polls have registered an extraordinarily high "favorability" rating for Trump among black voters—about 34-35 percent, far exceeding the 8 percent of the black electorate that actually voted for Trump in 2016. That's a huge jump from the 9 percent favorability rating among African Americans he earned in 2018 and the 13 percent he achieved earlier this year. [45]

Lawrence points out that a 35 percent favorability rating may not actually inspire 35 percent of black voters to cast ballots for Trump on Election Day, but even a small gain could give Republicans the margin of victory in key swing states like Pennsylvania and Michigan.

Three separate polls in late 2019 gave the president favorability ratings of 29 percent or higher among non-white voters. Among the general populace, July 2020 polls for the presidential race showed an even split between Trump and Biden.

TAKING IT TO THE STREETS

According to an article in *The New York Times*, during his "Black Voices for Trump" conference in Atlanta in November 2019, Trump told the audience, "We're going to campaign for every last African-American vote in 2020. We've done more for African-Americans in three years than the broken Washington establishment has done in more than 30 years." [46]

A journalist for *The New Yorker* covering the same event said Trump told the crowd, "Democrats are willing to destroy the foundations of our society and the pillars of our justice and judicial system in their craven pursuit of power and money," to which the crowd responded, "Amen." [47]

In an op-ed in the *Washington Examiner*, Vernon Robinson III and Bruce Eberle took notice of the steps Trump has already taken to address the interests of the black community:

Clearly, Trump's attention to black voters, his signing of the First Step prison reform bill, and his policies creating the lowest unemployment rate for black Americans in history have had an impact. Also important, a number of prominent black Americans who have moved from the Democratic Party to back

Trump, such as Candace Owens, and the recording star Kanye West, have not done so quietly, nor have they acted defensively. They have refused to be shamed into silence by the Democrats and the left-leaning news media. Instead, like their forbears in the civil rights movement of the 1950s and 60s, they have gone on offense, courageously exposing the fact that the policies of today's Democratic Party are often completely foreign to the values and aspirations of black Americans. [48]

Among the most notable African Americans who have abandoned the Democratic Party are Dr. Ben Carson, Supreme Court Justice Clarence Thomas, Heritage Foundation President Kay Cole James, Dr. Alveda King, businessman and former presidential candidate Herman Cain, and more than a dozen famous sports figures.

Robinson and Eberle concluded:

Current polls show black support for Trump approaching 30% — a dangerously high number for Democrats. If Trump wins even that much of the black vote, he will be reelected in a landslide. The movement of black Americans to Trump may not be as dramatic as the shift to FDR in 1936, but it may well be significant enough to create a red wave victory in 2020. [49]

Our future will be nothing if not exciting. As we close this chapter on traveling together, let me remind you that we are creating a new worldview and perspective that will allow minorities to help steer America to a new destination filled with liberty and justice for all.

We are creating a new worldview and perspective that will allow minorities to help steer America to a new destination filled with liberty and justice for all.

We have begun and ended every chapter of this book with lessons I learned from traveling with my family from Cincinnati to Norfolk, Virginia. The sense of family we created during those trips made it worth the effort.

From a comfort point of view, the first trip was probably the worst. My brother Eric and I were born less than two years apart; we seemingly alternated between laughing and joking to fighting and crying, all with equal intensity. My mother put her skills as a teacher to good use by creating games, reading stories, and, when necessary, acting as a referee when we fought. Despite our youth and our impatience, these trips brought me and Eric closer together. If our manifesto is going to work, we will have to purposely build bridges and trust the process.

After just a few annual summer sojourns, we knew our parents loved both of us, and an undying bond between us was forged and deepened.

In today's America, there is a great deal of anger erupting from numerous unexpected places. Only American Christians of different ethnicities can create the most direct path to unity. We will have to fight for a higher dimension of Christian harmony. There is multiplied power in agreement, as Jesus taught us:

Truly I tell you, whatever you bind on earth will be bound in heaven, and whatever you loose on earth will be loosed in heaven. Again, truly I tell you that if two of you on earth agree about anything they ask for, it will be done for them by my Father in heaven. For where two or three gather in my name, there am I with them. (Matthew 18:18–20)

Next, we are going to look at some of the easiest ways for our minorities to unite.

CHAPTER 6

CROSSING THE DIVIDE: SEVEN BRIDGES TO PEACE

Our trips to Virginia took a lot of planning and endurance for the drivers. The early-morning start was always grueling. My dad made sure he had a thermos full of coffee, my mom carefully packed the food, and their *human cargo*, me and my brother, were neatly settled in the back seat, where we would sleep for the first couple of hours. When we woke, we would excitedly observe the summer scenery.

About seven hours into the journey, we hit the bad spot. The roads to southern Virginia were narrow and often crowded. The worst part of the long day was a tunnel that took us under part of the Chesapeake Bay.

As my parents became more seasoned travelers, they learned that for a small fee, they could drive our car onto a sophisticated ferry and shorten our trip by nearly an hour. It was a godsend.

Jesus warned us that in the last days, nations (ethnic groups) would rise up against nations. (See Matthew 24:7.) In other words, we would see more intense ethnic conflicts.

What does this mean for Christians?

There are many divisions in personal, family, and national life that humanists and secular Americans cannot heal. In the last chapter, we approached fairness and reconciliation as though these were chiefly governmental issues. In this chapter, we will look at how we can build bridges of healing between the different ethnic groups within the American church.

For more than thirty years, I have shepherded a congregation of men and women from many racial and ethnic backgrounds who worship together as a unified body of believers. It was this solidarity that gave rise to a new reconciliation movement conceived as a multiracial expression of Christian faith, appealing to God through prayer and a rededication to reconciliation as a way to heal our land. When the founders and organizers of this new movement met, we did so in the belief that racism is America's *original sin*, present at the very beginning of our nation.

Too often throughout history, the Christian church has done too little to combat this grievous sin. Our goal was not to increase the level of acrimony and anger, either in the body of Christ or the culture at large, but to call for a new level of understanding and cooperation to bring the nation back to God and create an atmosphere of brotherhood and shared values for all our people.

As we began that series of meetings, the leaders—including me, Dr. James Robison, and Bishop T.D. Jakes—expressed our sorrow through repentance to the citizens of the United States that we had not done more to lead the way in healing our nation of the effects of intolerance and bigotry that arose from the sin of slavery. We believe that despite the courageous efforts of Christian abolitionists, civil rights leaders, and other social activists, the American church has never reached the critical level of engagement and unified action needed to end the reign of terror created by racism.

On January 15, 2015, we convened a historic meeting called "The Reconciled Church: Healing the Racial Divide." It's the name of the nonprofit organization that we cofounded while people were still fuming over the shooting death of Michael Brown, the African American man killed by a white police officer in Ferguson, Missouri. We convened the meeting to devise a plan that would say to the nation, "This is what we're doing to heal the racial divide in the church; let's use it to address systemic racism in our nation."

It's true that the body of Christ still has work to do, but the seven bridges to peace is a proven strategy for racial healing. We all agreed that in the heart of our God, the church is *already* one. Let's make it so in fact and deed! Martin Luther King Jr. called us "the beloved community." The only group capable of rising above the curse of racism and ethnic hatred is the Holy Spirit-empowered church.

Leaders of note who invested their time and resources for the meeting included: Robert Morris, Gateway Church; Ambassador Andrew Young; Dr. Alveda King, Priests for Life; Miles McPherson, Rock Church; Dr. A. R. Bernard, Christian Cultural Center; Dr. Tony Perkins, Family Research Council; Dr. Jack Graham, Prestonwood Baptist Church; John Hagee, Cornerstone Church; Bishop Paul Morton, founder of the Full Gospel Baptist Fellowship; Dr. Sammy Rodriguez, National Hispanic Christian Leadership Conference; Bishop Joseph Walker, Mt. Zion Baptist Church; Jim Daly, Focus on the Family; Leith Anderson, National Association of Evangelicals; Joshua DuBois, head of the White House Office of Faith-Based and Neighborhood Partnerships from 2009 to 2013; Stephen Strang, *Charisma* magazine; Dennis Rouse,

Victory Church; Jentezen Franklin, Free Chapel; Dr. Tony Evans, Oak Cliff Bible Fellowship; Steven Furtick, Elevation Church; and nearly two hundred other Christian leaders from all ethnicities, representing over forty million Christians.

More than seven thousand people attended the Thursday evening service at The Potter's House in Dallas, Texas. The event was also live-streamed and broadcast internationally by Daystar Television Network.

We believed that 2 Chronicles 7:14 provided the basis for believing that God can heal our individual hearts and help us unite to affect national renewal. We believed that true change must begin in the church and that it must be expressed locally. The Scripture says:

> If my people, who are called by my name, will humble themselves and pray and seek my face and turn from their wicked ways, then I will hear from heaven, and I will forgive their sin and will heal their land. (2 Chronicles 7:14)

As the chief convener of the movement, I shared our mission with these words:

> Recent polls show that given the current deterioration of race relations in our nation, especially in light of the Michael Brown and Eric Garner deaths, it is important for the church to lead the way in both racial reconciliation and societal reform. The conveners of this meeting believe that we can shift the racial atmosphere of the nation by healing the racial divisions in the church. Healing the racial divide in the nation will take the church's leadership. More specifically, we will need specific steps of action to heal the nation by engaging in seven spheres of activity. We strongly

believe that if the church takes unified action in real time, we can avert a national crisis and restore a sense of purpose and destiny to many individuals, their churches, and their communities. The root problems of America's ghettos are not unlike the problems of the nation's suburbs. Strangely enough, participating in the strategies that will bring a sense of justice to urban America will revitalize the Christian experience and devotion of suburban and affluent Christians as well.

Naturally, we need government, business, law enforcement, and community stakeholders to partner with us. However, we believe the glue that will keep our communities and our nation together will always be the church and its dedicated faith leaders. As we assembled our ideas and gained insight from those who had experience in these many areas, we drafted a list to indicate areas in which members of the Reconciled Church movement might become engaged.

Criminal justice reform seemed to be the most unifying step that we could take to build bridges for the church as a whole. During the January 2015 meeting, we discovered that all of us—blacks, whites, Hispanics, and Asians—felt that various reforms of our criminal justice system were urgently needed. Several of the conveners and attendees were among the nation's leading criminal justice reform advocates. The fact that the majority of incarcerated people are black or Hispanic is an indictment upon our justice system.

More than ten thousand people have graduated from Bishop Jakes's Texas Offenders Reentry Initiative (TORI). The program received an award from the Obama administration and is a model for regional reentry programs around the nation. Pat Nolan, director of the American Conservative Union Foundation's Center for Criminal Justice Reform, helped us draw white conservatives to stand shoulder to shoulder with liberal Christians to discuss the need to reform our criminal justice system. James Liske, then CEO of Prison Fellowship, was an articulate advocate in stressing the need for a unified approach to criminal justice reform.

Rounding out our criminal justice reform attendees was an organization called Right on Crime. For years, liberals have touted that they *own* the issue of criminal justice reform. Right on Crime appeared to be an oxymoron, like *a black conservative*. However, this group fights against over criminalization and supports juvenile justice, reducing recidivism rates, and preserving families.

As we left the meeting, we had a sense of expectation and hope. We conducted four more meetings with hundreds of pastoral leaders in Orlando, Florida; Montgomery, Alabama; Gainesville, Georgia; and Rock Hill, South Carolina.

In 2016, many of the participants in the Reconciled Church movement became advisors for the presidential campaigns of either Hillary Clinton or Donald Trump. I became a Trump supporter from the very beginning. By the time he was elected, there was an articulate, bipartisan, Christian movement that had chosen to advocate for criminal justice reform. I participated in and prayed publicly at President Trump's inaugural National Prayer Service at the National Cathedral on January 21, 2017.

Most of the people who were part of the Reconciled Church meeting two years prior went to work to get criminal justice reform high on the list of evangelical Christian priorities for the newly sworn-in administration. In less than two years, the Trump administration did what many felt was impossible, facilitating the passage of the First Step Act.

SEVEN BRIDGES TO PEACE

As I reflect on the first Reconciled Church meeting, I believe Bishop Jakes, James Robison, and I were fortunate to identify what we called *seven bridges to peace*. These are areas of participation that local churches can prioritize to heal the racial divide within their walls and in Christian parachurch initiatives. A small cluster of churches can make a huge impact when they invoke the power of agreement and unity.

American moral or governmental reform will only be as powerful as the church's resolve to organize, unify, and give leadership to the nation. Each bridge either brings internal unity across ethnic lines or gives focus and strategy for collaborative initiatives.

Prayer and Reconciliation Events

First, prayer will be perpetually offered to God to request His wisdom and divine aid for the multigenerational fulfillment of the Great Commandment and the Great Commission, respectively:

> *Love the Lord your God with all your heart and with all your soul and with all your mind and with all your strength.... Love your neighbor as yourself.* (Mark 12:30–31)

> *Go and make disciples of all nations, baptizing them in the name of the Father and of the Son and of the Holy Spirit, and teaching them to obey everything I have commanded you.* (Matthew 28:19–20)

We will have periodic interdenominational Christian gatherings with multiethnic believers to lift up specific areas of concern. This will be accompanied by periodic voluntary engagement in transparent, frank, civil, and godly dialogue to ensure agreement and coordination with all participants in this important plan. We will focus on implementation of plans of action to confront, overcome, and resolve destructive views, values, convictions, preferences, and practices—such as racism, sexism, and ageism—that divide the Lord's church, misrepresent Jesus Christ, defame God's creation, and hinder the fulfillment of the Great Commandment and the Great Commission.

These prayer and fellowship events are not meant as *Kumbaya* events that create warm, fuzzy feelings without a commitment to social or political change. Instead, they will create the relational equity that we can draw upon in the years ahead, when decisive action is needed.

Education Reform

Serious attention must be given to increasing access to early educational programs prior to kindergarten. By the third grade, minority students are often significantly behind their white counterparts. These same kids are sometimes labeled as learning disabled or prison-bound. After-school tutorial programs, charter schools, and religious-based elementary schools could turn around minority underachievement in just a decade or so. Churches can also play a major role in offering academic and character-building enrichment programs to students of middle and high school age. The focus will be on developing skills in core academic subjects, including language, science, math, and Christian faith and values.

If these measures are taken seriously, minority college dropout rates will also sharply decline in just a few years. Education is still a pathway to the top for *"the least of these"* (Matthew 25:40) in our culture.

Civic Engagement

These meetings would emphasize Christian citizenship training, best practices for dealing with law enforcement, civil rights, and other social or political issues that may denigrate individuals and threaten their quality of life. For example, citizens should feel empowered to exercise their right to vote and participate in jury duty, community outreach, school, library, and children's programs, town councils, and groups such as their local Parent-Teacher Association. In a post-COVID-19 era, public health meetings, financial strategy sessions, and career coaching will be important ways a multiple church collaboration could serve our cities and states.

Community Outreach and Service

Christian faith-based interdenominational and multiethnic churches must provide compassionate outreach with various kinds of social services. These are strategic efforts to serve the under-resourced and poverty-stricken residents living in the economically distressed and financially depressed zones of the urban community. We can gain from the experience of Christian groups in St. Louis and other urban centers, which offer models for counseling, legal representation, financial assistance, housing, education, healthcare programs, and employment training, among other areas.

Marriage and Family

We need programs and services that will help to introduce, rebuild, restore, and enhance the sanctity of life, the discovery of personal and relational identity, and an understanding of God's provision of purpose and destiny for our lives. Navigation into the discovery and the fulfillment of these can come through seminars, personal and group counseling, youth athletic programs, pro-life services, and biblical marriage and family training programs. Mentoring and fatherhood initiatives should be a key component of this bridge to peace.

Advocacy for the Unborn

The church is not called to be a mouthpiece for any political party; rather, it is to be a moral example to the nation. Our society is in desperate need of moral guidance that Christians can provide in a public role that stirs the national conscience. When Dr. Tony Perkins and I joined together in the opening hours of the Obama administration to write the book *Personal Faith, Public Policy,* [50] our goal was to offer Christians of all social and racial backgrounds a set of guidelines for living their lives faithfully as Christians and responsible members of society.

To be a responsible Christian means to remain faithful to the principles of Scripture and the character of Jesus Christ. Being part of a church, a political party, or a movement of any kind is not the same as being personally devoted to a morally responsible way of life. As much good as the so-called *religious right* may have done over the past three decades, it's unfortunate that it's been branded as an appendage of the Republican Party rather than as faithful ambassadors of Christ. Politics are important, and we ought to be engaged, but our political choices must be tempered by a Christian political agenda and the truth of the gospel message.

Those who label themselves *independents* or *moderates* may say that in order to be ambassadors for Christ, we must withdraw from the political process, but I wholeheartedly reject that idea. Consider what the silence of Christians has done over the last fifty years and consider the difference we might have made if the church had stood up to block the Supreme

Court's odious *Roe v. Wade* decision in 1973. Instead, the church was silent—and the lives of more than 63 million innocent children have been lost, including more than 19 million African Americans.

As our culture has sunk lower into an immoral secular abyss, the world needs the Christian voice to resonate once again and call the nations back to God. Rather than silence, we need action. Evangelicals in the past have tolerated character flaws and incompetence in their leaders and rejected certain candidates because their friends or social role models condemned them. But Hollywood will always make outcasts of moral and religious people. And nothing so condemns the left's thinking than the sin of abortion. If we ever hope to serve God with all of our hearts, this is one cause that no serious follower of Jesus Christ can afford to ignore. And that's just one part of the battle we're in.

Criminal Justice Reform

Minority engagement with the criminal justice system is at the core of our current tensions in the black community. We need strategic involvement to bring about real reform. This would include training for prison and jail evangelism workers, and regional partnerships for prison aftercare and job creation. Programs like those being offered by the Prison Fellowship can provide models, instruction, and guidance for civic engagement on these issues. This is an area that is being actively pursued at the national level by the White House and by civic and religious groups nationwide. Recent legislation has brought about better and more realistic sentencing guidelines for nonviolent offenders. In an upcoming chapter, I will share the incredible story of Catherine Toney, who gives us a perfect example of what can happen when mercy meets criminal justice reform.

Economic Development

In addition to personal financial training, credit repair, and benevolence, many other dimensions of economic equipping can be launched from our churches. Investment training, schools of business, and specific entrepreneurial training plans can be developed through the resources of lay persons and others in the community with expertise in finance and economics. There are several different models from St. Louis and other large urban centers that will help to position the church to encourage a better understanding of *ethical capitalism*.

A PERSONAL CHALLENGE

There is only so much our public servants can do to address the individual and institutional needs in our communities. As I've argued throughout these pages, we must be vigilant and thoughtful in choosing the men and women whom we elect to represent us on the local, state, and national levels. Additionally, we must be diligent in working for the betterment of our cities and towns by reaching out through programs like the aforementioned.

We cannot be all things to all people. None of us can do all of these things alone. But we *can* each do *something*. We can each find places to serve, whether in the local church, our municipality, or a nonprofit organization that's truly making a difference. My challenge to each reader is to think prayerfully about what you *can* do, speak with others who feel as you do, and take positive steps to become a change agent in your community.

THE TIPPING POINT

Jesus's commandment for us to love one another may be the hardest to keep, and the history of our people would suggest it may be impossible. But if it could not be done, Christ would never have told us to do it. If we are willing to learn from our mistakes and look for new ways to work together, I believe miracles can happen. Communities can live together in peace if our doors and our hearts are open to change. There is good sociological evidence for this in Malcolm Gladwell's best-selling book, *The Tipping Point*, which discusses how revolutionary changes take place in the natural order. [51]

Gladwell shows how cultural trends change suddenly and dramatically when the right circumstances and players are in place. There are many factors that can set off a sudden change response: we see it in medicine, psychology, and especially in business, where a new fad can suddenly spread like wildfire. However, there are common factors in every case. When the environment is right, anything can change, suddenly and dramatically.

For years, the underlying message from the left has been that blacks and other minorities can't possibly make it on their own. They insinuate that white culture is out to get minorities and the latter need to stay with "our people," as the left creates an us-versus-them mentality. Most of all, minorities are supposed to keep the self-appointed gatekeepers in power and the rest of the nation in turmoil to ensure that minorities get their "rights."

Conservatives, on the other hand, believe in the power of personal responsibility and self-determination. We believe that individuals, free from government interference and restrictions, can rise above their circumstances through hard work and self-discipline. The race hustlers tell us that conservatives are against the poor, but that is not true. A vast amount of research data shows that conservatives are more generous in their charitable giving than liberals, and Christian conservatives are the most generous of all.

More importantly, conservatives believe that free enterprise, wealth creation, and upward mobility are every person's right and privilege. Those things cannot be mandated by government; they come through the dignity of work. Clearly, the messages of the left and the right are in conflict, and a lot of people in our communities are stuck somewhere in between. We want to make our own way in the world and achieve great things, but we have been told that Uncle Sam is our only hope. We are told that Republicans don't care about poor people.

Yet, instead of doing things to simplify our lives and remove the roadblocks that prevent our people from getting ahead, Democrats spend their time passing unconstructive bills like increasing the minimum wage, as if that will solve all problems. Sorry, but the minimum wage is designed for teenagers and workers with minimum skills. Is that the best they can do? Giving a *tip* to people on the bottom rung of the economic ladder will not change conditions in the ghetto. Ghettos can only be changed by the moral renewal that happens within each individual human heart and by economic development that creates middle-class jobs and viable industries. Two years from now, all the effort spent on raising the minimum wage will not have any significance. Instead, like the old Wendy's commercial, we will be yelling, "Where's the beef?"

A few years ago, feminists were talking about breaking through the glass ceiling into corporate management. The media blew it up and tried to make corporate America the villain, saying they were holding back a generation of female executives. It turned out, however, that the only barrier holding women back was their own lack of preparation. When women who were motivated to enter the world of big business got the education and experience they needed to apply for those jobs, they got their shot. Today, some of the most accomplished and highest paid executives in the country are women. And, believe me, those women earned those jobs by proving they could do the work, not by government mandates.

This is happening in the black community as well. By way of example, look at Herman Cain, the founder of Godfather's Pizza and an accomplished black business consultant who achieved success based on his own fortitude and imagination. Such people aren't asking for handouts. They have broken through the racial glass ceiling and earned their success the old-fashioned way. Growing numbers of blacks hold positions as executives, mid-level managers, doctors, lawyers, and professionals in many fields. They are making a contribution to the community and are visible examples of what motivated people can achieve. To break free, we have to forget the labels and stereotypes that liberals have been putting on us for years.

THE POWER OF TRANSFORMATION

We need to understand that the tax-and-spend Democrats have not changed their stripes. The money they are spending comes out of your pocket, too. If our people are content to live on handouts from government welfare, we will be defined by our poverty. But if we want to be defined by our skills and talents, then we need to start associating with people who believe in the benefits of free enterprise, personal responsibility, and prosperity.

Blacks and whites have to come together. For their part, whites need to take steps to cross the racial divide. They need to be willing to work with and for blacks in business, and they need to elect more qualified blacks to public office. On the other hand, there will have to be some fundamental rethinking in the black community, too, especially about how long we intend to live under the thumb of politicians who are busy making life more comfortable for us at the bottom rung of society instead of making a place for us in the upper ranks.

The social programs of the 1960s worked against us, and all the hot-button issues I have addressed are part of the Sixties' residue. Conservative Christians know that the federal government cannot change the evil nature of man. Only the gospel of Jesus Christ can change a human heart; everything else is a temporary measure. Today, in the midst of one of the most contentious and politically agitated times in our lives, and in the shadow of a failed impeachment attempt on the president of the United States, blacks and whites will have to discover the benefits of working together for our mutual benefit, or the chaos will only grow more intense and more unsettling.

The fact that between 10 and 20 percent of African Americans are willing to take a second look at their bondage to the Democratic Party, voting for morally responsible conservative candidates, is a great start. The biggest sociological change of all may not be far behind. When we have a majority of the principled, hard-working men and women in our communities, empowered by their faith in God and a commitment to personal responsibility, we will truly have reached a tipping point. And that is something to look forward to.

I want to end this chapter with the declaration that the church is going to win the war against racism and hate. It may take many years for America to become truly ethnically mixed. If churches evangelize and disciple their people biblically, the next great awakening will sweep us into a dynamic, empowering unity. As Dr. King stated with a spiritual wisdom beyond his years, "Darkness cannot drive out darkness: only light can do that."

As I return to my family's annual summer trip, I recall how close my brother and I became thanks to those journeys. We both learned what it meant to be a Jackson and I learned that Eric had a more technical mind than I did, which eventually led to a career working with computers for Procter & Gamble. The net result was that during our journeys, we grew up and we grew together.

In the next chapter, we are going to drill down on the reasons why the Hispanic community will benefit from multiplying its influence through spiritually grounded unity. Blacks and Asians need the strengths that the Hispanic community brings to the table.

CHAPTER 7

PASSING THE HISPANIC AND ASIAN DRIVER'S TEST

When I started playing high school football, my summer-long family excursions ceased. Nevertheless, we took some shorter trips back to our family capital of Norfolk. During those later trips, my brother and I were able to drive—under the strict scrutiny of our parents, of course. Although we had valid driver's licenses, my dad had to feel comfortable releasing the wheel. As we moved into adulthood, we became full-fledged members of the travel team. Whenever there was a graduation, a sick relative, or funeral, a travel team was recruited. After my father died, my trips became less frequent. We would simply rendezvous in Norfolk. I would often come from Washington, Philadelphia, or Cleveland, and my mother would travel from DC. As we apply this analogy to bringing our nation together, let's consider the Hispanic population.

Close to sixty million Hispanics live in the U.S., making them the largest minority in the country. [52] But minority groups don't vote the same on every issue, and one need look no further than Hispanic evangelicals to substantiate that claim.

This powerful voting bloc can catapult a campaign to victory or sink it, no matter whether the candidate is Democrat or Republican.

For instance, an impressive 41 percent of Hispanic evangelicals voted for President Trump in 2016, *Christianity Today* reported. The results found that while many Christians voted for Trump, they did so for different reasons: "Nineteen percent said improving the economy, 14 percent said helping those in need, and 14 percent said a candidate's position on immigration," the report revealed. [53]

The data is good news for conservatives, but understanding why Hispanics vote the way they do is important because they could determine who wins the White House in November, especially in conservative-leaning swing states. The fact is, our Hispanic brothers and sisters are crucial to the preservation of Christian values in the United States, and Republicans would be wise to engage this important demographic.

Our Hispanic brothers and sisters are crucial to the preservation of Christian values in the United States.

HE'S ON THE LORD'S SIDE

When it comes to speaking up for pro-family and Christian values and representing Hispanic Christians around the world, no better example exists than Rev. Samuel Rodriguez. The president of the National Hispanic Christian Leadership Conference (NHCLC) has been a tireless advocate for Hispanic evangelicals. While media organizations often paint Hispanics as a monolithic, pro-Democratic Party constituency, Rodriguez reminds friend and foe alike that there is no more conservative, pro-life voice in America than the millions who identify with the NHCLC.

This is significant in light of Rodriguez's regular meetings with members of both parties in Congress and service with Presidents George W. Bush, Barack Obama, and Donald Trump. In 2016, when a California state senator proposed a bill outlawing discrimination in higher education because of sexual orientation—which would have scuttled the state's exemption for religious schools from such requirements—the NHCLC successfully opposed it. The group's national profile and widespread credibility helped to create a new partnership with Oral Roberts University to equip the next generation of Hispanic evangelicals for ministry. NHCLC is also training millennials to take a stand for God.

Rodriguez told me he has a strategy to engage millennials in the upcoming election. "NHCLC launched a campaign called Free to Preach, with the objective to preach in cities, but not just preach," he says. "We're going to have large rallies in states across America, primarily swing states, after the coronavirus issue.

"The objective is to have millennials make an agreement with God that they will only vote life, religious liberty, and biblical justice, meaning they will not support any candidate, party, or ideology that is not committed to doing biblical justice in the name of Jesus," Rodriguez explains.

The top priority for the National Hispanic Christian Leadership Conference is standing up for the unborn.

There are numerous issues that resonate with Hispanic evangelicals, but the top priority for NHCLC is standing up for the unborn, followed closely by religious liberty and biblical justice.

Rodriguez says 54 percent of Hispanic millennials believe abortion should be illegal in most or all cases, according to a 2015 Pew Research study. More than 25 percent of Hispanics consider abortion to be the critical issue that determines how they vote. "It was the largest percentage of all ethnicities, including white evangelicals," Rodriguez says. [54]

A GODLY AGENDA

When asked why religious liberty is a top priority, Rodriguez points to the past. "Many Latinos migrated from socialist, totalitarian, and authoritarian regimes that stifled religious liberty and religious expression," he explains. Since generations of Hispanics were forbidden to exercise their faith and worship freely, NHCLC is working to prevent that from ever happening again.

The third issue important to Hispanic Christians is biblical justice, which gets its meaning from Micah 6:8: *"He has shown you, O mortal, what is good. And what does the LORD require of you? To act justly and to love mercy and to walk humbly with your God."* It is under the umbrella of biblical justice that NHCLC addresses issues such as comprehensive immigration reform, education, human trafficking, and poverty, all from a biblical approach.

Rodriguez has also written several books, including *When Faith Catches Fire*, [55] chronicling the passion and fire of the Latino community, which he believes will bring a new reformation to the United States.

Rodriguez further positioned himself to speak up for biblical justice on a national platform during an interview with *Fox News* after he visited a migrant facility in Clint, Texas.

"I'm not a Republican or a Democrat. I'm a Christian committed to righteousness and justice," he remarked. "Congress is playing politics with millions of individuals, with the sovereignty of our nation, and with the protection of our border." [56]

Rodriguez said while Democratic Congresswoman Alexandria Ocasio-Cortez blamed Republicans for what she said were deplorable conditions at the facility, he found "no soiled diapers, no deplorable conditions, and no lack of basic necessities." In fact, many of the Border Patrol and immigration officers are Latino, he noted. One emotional Border Patrol agent told him, "Pastor Sam, what they're saying about us is completely false. We care about these kids and have a passion for our calling." [57]

Hispanic evangelicals are "prophetically progressive" when it comes to taking care of the poor.

Rodriguez notes Hispanic evangelicals are conservative about social issues and "prophetically progressive" when it comes to taking care of the poor. "There are items within the Democratic Party that resonate every time you talk about them, like climate change or student loan debt, healthcare, and education. But it's not a Republican or Democrat agenda that's most important. They are not married to the agenda of the donkey or the elephant. It's the Lamb's agenda that matters most." [58]

HISPANICS TAKE THE WHEEL

Just as I had to grow up and share in the responsibilities of driving my parents and brother on those road trips, all minority communities must understand that we have to take the wheel and drive the car! Slick political candidates who talk a lot, but produce little to nothing at all, will no longer patronize minority voters without suffering political consequences. Our concerns must be the priority of both parties.

For instance, education, wealth creation, and entrepreneurship are all tangible reasons why we need to coalesce as a voting bloc to ensure that our concerns are included in the national platforms of both the Democratic and Republican parties. We must send a message that a left versus right mentality is outdated and, in some ways, racist.

This may come as a surprise to some people, but conservatism doesn't make a person a Christian any more than drinking milk makes them a cow. Therefore, conservatism alone can't be the standard by which minority groups devise a strategy to influence politics in this country. If we want God to bless our nation, righteousness and justice must be the determining factor in how we select one candidate or another.

Voters can be intentional about their spiritual walk and civic responsibility through alignment, intercession, and mobilization.

AIM HIGH WHEN YOU VOTE

I'd like to see Hispanics and Asian Americans vote in historically high numbers, but with a purpose. I want them to *AIM* high! AIM is an acrostic that I created to help voters be intentional about their spiritual walk and civic responsibility. It stands for:

+ *Alignment:* Come under spiritual authority by joining a local church

+ *Intercession:* Pray for education reform, marriage rebuilding, minority and community engagement, wealth creation, entrepreneurship, righteousness and justice, empathy versus retaliation, and destiny with dignity.

+ *Mobilization:* Organize spiritually and naturally to participate in the vote, platform committees, and other avenues of citizen leadership.

Hispanics must hold both parties accountable by leveraging their influence to address practical issues. Both parties can start by answering questions such as:

What will Democrats and Republicans do to address the disparity in home ownership among Hispanics? Even though home ownership is on the rise in Latino communities, it's not where it should be if we are honest with ourselves.

What will be done to close the educational gap between Hispanic children and their counterparts?

Is a bipartisan response to the immigration problem too much to ask? Immigration has been overshadowed in recent months by the onslaught of COVID-19, but the issue will be in the minds of millions of Hispanics when they march into the voting booth to exact justice on the candidate who failed to provide acceptable solutions to immigration.

I believe Hispanics have the ability to drive the 2020 presidential election, but both political parties had better bring more than broken promises if they want the Latino vote. And I'm certainly not alone in my thinking.

"We're pro-life. We want criminal justice reform. We want educational equity. We want a healthy economy," the Rev. Gabriel Salguero, president of the National Latino Evangelical Coalition, told *Religion News Service*. He notes that immigration and foreign policy are also key concerns. "Because we're not one-issue voters, people think if they come to us with talking points they're gonna get us—no. ... They need to have a holistic agenda that addresses the variety of issues that are important to us, both as evangelicals and Hispanics." [59]

THE ASIAN EQUATION

They often go unnoticed in the political process, but as the fourth largest racial group in the U.S.—and the fastest growing—the Asian American population could prove pivotal in determining who wins in November. This is why I believe that we conservatives must pay attention and court this key voting demographic.

The Asian American population could prove pivotal in determining who wins the 2020 presidential election.

More than eleven million Asian Americans will be eligible to vote this year, or nearly 5 percent of the electorate. From 2000 to 2020, the number of Asian American eligible voters more than doubled, growing by 139 percent. At the same time, the Hispanic electorate grew by 121 percent, while the black and white electorates grew by 33 percent and 7 percent, respectively. [60]

The Asian vote is now large enough to make or break an election in a couple battleground states. Fortunately, some Asian leaders are reaching out to potential voters to make it happen.

It's also a historic moment in politics for candidates of Asian descent. Though they since have dropped out of the race, three people of Asian-Pacific descent campaigned for the Democratic nomination for president: entrepreneur Andrew Yang, California Senator Kamala Harris, and Hawaii Representative Tulsi Gabbard. Such participation underscores the need for the Republican Party to increase its efforts to engage the Asian voting bloc—and there's no time like the present.

Given President Trump's tax-cutting, deregulatory policies, and the fact that many Asian Americans see affirmative action policies as stacked against them, I find it puzzling that just 18 percent of Asian Americans voted for President Trump in 2016, according to one exit poll. [61]

According to *The Washington Post*, Asian Americans faithfully vote Democratic. "Sixty-five percent of Asian Americans are Democrats or lean toward the Democratic Party, while only 27 percent identify as a Republican or lean toward the GOP." [62]

Quite presciently, the *Post* adds: "Yet they're often relegated to, at best, a footnote in conversations about national politics." [63]

However, former Texas pastor Herman Martir believes there is about to be a shift among Asian Americans, whom he sees helping to reelect Trump. The one-time leader of a multicultural church and a member of the president's Advisory Commission on Asian Americans and Pacific Islanders, the Fort Worth leader has a keen sense of the Asian electorate.

"I believe that Asian Americans are waking up to the reality that under President Trump's administration, Asian American employment has increased to the highest level and this employment increase is the highest in history," Martir told me. "And the unemployment also is at a record low, and the Asian American business community and the faith community believe in his conservative agenda."

THE TRUMP EFFECT

Miki Carver, Asian Pacific American press secretary for the Republican National Committee, echoed Martir's point in an interview with *USA Today*. Carver predicted that Asian Americans would vote for President Trump because of a strong economy under his administration, not because of skin color.

"I don't really see this as only voting for somebody because of their race, but based on their agenda, and we have a results-driven economy right now," she explained. "And I think that's what's resonating with everybody." [64]

Although Asian Americans represent a diverse population, as a whole, they typically have conservative values.

As is true of Hispanics, it is worth pointing out that that Asian Americans represent a diverse population, composed of different nationalities, races, cultures, and religions. Still, they typically support free enterprise, traditional family values, personal responsibility, education, and hard work, the *National Review* reported [65]—all of which makes them a perfect fit for the Republican Party.

Indeed, during an interview for this book, Martir confirmed what I have suspected for some time now: there is growing support among the Asian American community for President Trump's policies and agenda.

"I believe that the president wants to represent or include all Americans, not just a small segment of our communities," Martir said. "As Asian Americans, we believe in conservative values. We're pro-family and pro-business. We believe in hard work and self-reliance. So we are a natural fit when it comes to the policy and the agenda that the president has set for America."

While a small minority of Asian Americans were registered to vote, according to the U.S. Census, Martir sees that changing rapidly. He serves as president of the Asian Action Network, which represents six thousand pastors, churches, and nonprofit organizations dedicated to building strong families and communities through faith-based and neighborhood initiatives. For me, this reiterates the fact that he knows the heartbeat of Asian voters.

He told followers of his blog that Asian Americans and Pacific Islanders are now the fastest growing racial group in the United States, increasing over four times as rapidly as the total U.S. population and expected to double from 20 million to more than 47 million by 2060. Although many Asians voted for Hillary Clinton in 2016, Martir notes more are registering as Republicans.

"I know for a fact that there is an awakening when it comes to the faith community," Martir says. "We mobilized thousands of churches to vote and we are doing the same thing for this coming election. We're seeing a tremendous support when it comes to President Trump's agenda. Asian Americans and Pacific Islanders will be, I believe, the swing votes for key battleground states."

ASIAN AMERICANS IN THE DRIVER'S SEAT

Martir is on the frontlines when it comes to Asian American voters, traveling nationwide to engage Asian citizens, pastors, and leaders. His regular meetings, roundtable discussions, voter education drives, and conference calls make him confident that Asian Americans will change the heretofore common statistical voting profile—not based on wishful thinking, but because of their status as the fastest-growing racial group, the most highly educated group, and the highest income group of American minorities.

"There are a lot of positives pointing to the right direction," says Martir, stressing it is a new day for Asian Americans. "In the past, they were solicited by political parties on every election and many of them vote for those candidates and politicians. But in the end, they have been completely ignored after the election."

Asian Americans have increasingly become Trump supporters in key battleground states.

Asian Americans have increasingly become Trump supporters in key battleground states such as Nevada, Florida, Pennsylvania, and Virginia. Even in Texas and Minnesota, they are doing voter engagement with numerous faith and minority communities—and finding willing listeners.

Regardless of how the presidential election goes, Martir is confident that Asian Americans will play a large role in 2020 as they become a crucial voting bloc in swing states.

"That's why I believe that we will surprise the nation come November because many of them right now are saying, 'We want to get involved; we want to be part of the political system in America and we want to be represented,'" he observes. "Many of them, in fact, want to run for political office. So that's why I feel that there's a strong swing towards that."

Besides Martir, I see other rising voices in the Asian American community, including Republican congressional candidate Young Kim of California, Utah Attorney General Sean Reyes, and Mayor Ron Falconi of Brunswick, Ohio. Like Martir, Reyes and Falconi have served on Trump's Advisory Commission on Asian Americans and Pacific Islanders.

Falconi has been tapped by the Republican National Convention to reach out to Asian American voters in his key battleground state. In October 2019, he told a reporter that in the end, people will ask themselves whether they are better off now than they were four years ago.

"And I think our economy is doing well, this president has had the lowest Asian American unemployment, lowest Hispanic unemployment, the lowest African American unemployment," Falconi said. "A lot of times people vote for their pocketbooks and right now the economy is doing well and I think it's going to be an easy sell." [66]

Like Falconi and Martir, I agree that Asian Americans have a lot to like about the Trump administration. This was spotlighted on January 27, 2020, when Vice President Mike Pence administered the oath of office to the new members of the Asian Advisory Commission at the White House in celebration of the Lunar New Year. Pence said:

> This year we've got a lot to celebrate. … Asian Americans are prospering like never before, and the American economy is booming. In fact, Americans of Asian and Pacific Island descent are the fastest-growing group in America—growing by nearly three-quarters in just 15 years, and expected to double over the next 40 years. And, in fact, according to the Census Bureau, household income for Asian Americans is now 40 percent higher than the national average, and rising fast. The American economy is soaring, and Asian Americans are driving capital investment and growth and job creation in cities and towns, large and small, all across the land. [67]

Clearly, Asian Americans are not a group that should be a footnote in the national political discussion.

FOCUSING ON WHAT'S IMPORTANT

One of the problems my brother and I had on our Virginia excursions was our tendency to bicker over inconsequential things. We would fight over our toys, hit one another, complain to our parents about what the other was doing, and tattle on each other. All of a sudden, my mother would transform from teacher to judge. While Dad had mastered the art of tuning us out, Mom felt the need to settle us down. I can only imagine what a large family would do on such a trip! Every year, Mom would simply modify the rules. The first rule was no hitting; the second rule was no name calling. The older we got, the more sophisticated the rules or guidelines became.

As we continue our *Manifesto* journey, we must decide how to create the appropriate tension between righteousness and justice, particularly the need for minority and white Christians to think more biblically about these terms and how they apply to our culture.

CHAPTER 8

THE DESTINATION: BIBLICAL JUSTICE AND RIGHTEOUSNESS

As we grew older, my mother told Eric and me more stories about black history. We learned all the great things that black people had done, things they created, and values that great black leaders had espoused. Our discussions became more thoughtful and focused. My mother had a heart full of compassion and loved to express that love in practical ways. In her mind, the Bible was all about the tension between mercy and holiness.

My goal in this chapter is to lay out my understanding of the biblical concepts of righteousness and justice and how they apply to our culture and politics.

MOUNTAIN-MOVING FAITH

When we Christians fuse our faith with good works, we can ignite a movement. Catherine Toney is the perfect example of what it means for the church to go beyond our immaculate sanctuaries to transform the lives of people in this country.

Toney was sentenced to twenty years in federal prison after being found guilty of "conspiracy to possess with the intent to distribute cocaine base." [68] If you were to talk with her, she would readily admit that what she did was wrong, but some lawmakers believed that nonviolent offenders like Toney were often over-sentenced. The shift in thinking led to aggressive criminal justice reform, and God opened the door for ministry leaders to help craft the bill.

After serving sixteen long years, Toney, now age fifty-five, walked out of a Florida prison a free woman in 2019 because Republicans, Democrats, the Reconciled Church, and others joined forces to pass the First Step Act (FSA). The bill, which President Trump signed into law in 2018, was designed "to improve criminal justice outcomes, as well as to reduce the size of the federal prison population while also creating mechanisms to maintain public safety." [69]

All believers in Christ Jesus are called to put their faith into action in some area of society.

It is my conviction that all believers in Christ Jesus are called to put their faith into action in some area of society. Jesus said those who help people in need, including prisoners, will be richly rewarded in the kingdom of heaven.

> *The King will say to those on his right, "Come, you who are blessed by my Father; take your inheritance, the kingdom prepared for you since the creation of the world. For I was hungry and you gave me something to eat, I*

was thirsty and you gave me something to drink, I was a stranger and you invited me in, I needed clothes and you clothed me, I was sick and you looked after me, I was in prison and you came to visit me." (Matthew 25:34–36)

I got involved in Toney's case because I believed she was one of the people in prison about whom Jesus spoke. A couple days after her release, she was whisked off to the White House to give a speech on what it meant to be a recipient of the new law. When I walked up to congratulate her and ask how things were going, she lowered her voice and told me she didn't really have any clothes.

"I don't have anything," she said. "I need a job, but I don't have the clothes I need to go find a job. I don't have any of the basic essentials that I need."

We were standing in the most famous house in the nation, yet Toney didn't have what she needed to live once she left there. President Trump's son-in-law, Jared Kushner, made a phone call and got her a job at the local Walmart in her hometown of Mobile, Alabama, so that was no longer a problem. But how was she going to get back and forth to work without a car?

When Toney told me about everything she was dealing with, I didn't hesitate to help her. I returned home from the event and made some calls. As a result, Bishop David Richey of Birmingham, Bishop Kyle Searcy of Fresh Anointing House of Worship in Montgomery, Dr. Sharon Nesbitt of Dominion Church in Marion, Arkansas, and I each chipped in a thousand dollars to buy a car for Toney. It was enough money to pay for a nice used car, car insurance, and the vehicle registration fee.

I interviewed Toney for this book, so I'd like to let her tell you, in her own words, how her life was transformed by the power and grace of God:

> I was the first woman to be released from prison under the First Step Act. And two and a half days after my release in April 2019, I was invited to the White House, where I spoke at an event along with President Trump. I talked about how grateful I was to be home with my daughter and granddaughter and my other family members. I thanked the president, Jared Kushner, the organization Cut 50 with Van Jones, and Bishop Harry Jackson. I was released because of their hard work. They helped put the bill together. After I greeted everybody, I told Bishop Jackson I had nothing. I left prison with no clothes or the essentials that I needed. I told him I still had a mountain to climb. He gave me a card and said, "Call me because my church and organization, we do things like this, we help people like yourself." I called the next day, and the first thing the bishop did was send me a thousand dollars so I could get me some clothes and other essentials. Three weeks later, he called and said, "Meet Bishop Richey, pastor of Gulf Coast Christian Center in Mobile, Alabama, and pick up your car." I met him at the car lot, and they presented me with a car! I thank God for Bishop Jackson for giving me that little bit of hope from the beginning when I got out.

I'm not sharing this story because I'm seeking personal applause, but to give God the glory for giving a new life to a former inmate, and to illustrate how Christians can be politically engaged without compromising our faith. Imagine what would happen if every Christian church in the U.S. adopted someone who had just been released from jail or prison. Prisons would report lower recidivism rates, the gospel message would increase, and God would be glorified.

Imagine what would happen if every Christian church in the U.S. adopted someone who had just been released from jail or prison.

SIGNS OF RESTORATION

In 1906, there was a major spiritual awakening in America that changed the nation's religious destiny when the Spirit of God moved upon William Seymour in a dynamic way. It was clear that he had been blessed with a powerful anointing. Thus was born the Azusa Street Revival.

Before long, people from all over the world, both black and white, came to Seymour and experienced a fresh touch from God. The meetings he held were marked by an unusual unity. Amazingly, this move of God was led by a handicapped black man who came from a very poor family. Some have said this revival was a foreshadowing of Dr. Martin Luther King's dream for America.

During the Great Depression, African Americans were once again a moral lightning rod. My book with George Barna entitled *High-Impact African American Churches* [70] includes the story of an African American dentist from Poughkeepsie, New York, who gathered together a consortium of black churches for vocational training. The black church challenged the prevailing thinking of the day that blacks were only fit for menial jobs.

Blacks once again became a moral compass for America during the 1950s and 1960s. The civil rights movement, which began with Rosa Parks in December 1955, was led by local black pastors and Christian leaders who made a commitment to change America through nonviolence. Martin Luther King Jr. and many others articulated a dream that was for *all* Americans, not black people alone. Today, that moral lightning rod remains in place as the black community is being used to bring a word from God for the nation. But to hear this word, the nation needs a better understanding of this community.

The landscape of African American life is changing quickly. There is an emerging black middle class that needs to understand economics and how to run businesses. At the same time, the black community is suffering from a dangerous disintegration of the nuclear family. Two-thirds of black babies born in America this year will be born without a father in the home. Further, there is an alarming rate of HIV/AIDS and addictive behaviors that seem to prey on the young and the most socially vulnerable.

There are numerous problems related to the disturbing number of African American males in prisons. As the church speaks out and deals with these issues in practical ways, Christians will ignite a movement to release the justice of God in our country. I believe the Lord will use the plight of African Americans to reveal His own glory. Men and women of faith need to rise up and pursue righteousness and justice as the Lord leads. I believe that as God deals with the problems of black America, the overflow of His grace and bounty will impact the nation as a whole.

As God deals with the problems of black America, the overflow of His grace and bounty will impact the nation as a whole.

DELIVERING THE MESSAGE

To set the stage for a bold cultural movement, I gathered a group of gifted pastors and teachers to call upon Christian leaders from many backgrounds to form a new multigenerational team of thought leaders who will seek to transform a small conservative fringe into a registered voting bloc of African Americans, Hispanics, Asians, and other first-generation immigrants who are prepared to challenge the status quo and stand firm for our shared values based on biblical principles and common sense.

The economic, moral, and social interests of African Americans run parallel with the values of Christian believers everywhere. Our Sunday services may look different, and our expressions of faith and worship may differ, but the unifying philosophical thread that has bound men and women of all ethnic and cultural backgrounds together throughout most of our history is what historians call *the faith of our fathers*—the ideals that allowed the nation to prosper.

Although we have strayed from those ideals, this nation was built by a coalition of far-sighted individuals united by biblical concepts of righteousness and justice. Psalm 89:14–15 (NKJV) puts it very well: *"Righteousness and justice are the foundation of Your throne; mercy and truth go before Your face. Blessed are the people who know the joyful sound!"*

America has prospered as no other nation; we've enjoyed the blessings of heaven throughout most of our history. Like every nation, we've endured many failures and lapses of judgment that demand repentance, but the psalmist also says, *"Blessed is the nation whose God is the LORD"* (Psalm 33:12), and that ought to be the hope that guides us.

Prior to the 2004 presidential election, a group called the Ohio Election Center commissioned a study to measure the values of registered voters. What they found was that the black community was predominantly pro-family and against same-sex marriage; by a small margin, they supported the social policies of the Republicans. [71]

For generations, black voters felt locked into supporting Democrats, even when the party's political agenda was incompatible with their values.

For generations, black voters felt locked into supporting Democrats, even when the party's political agenda was incompatible with the values of the black community. The only ones in favor of our pro-life, pro-family, and faith-friendly agenda were the Republicans. This was eye-opening for many of us, and that was when I saw the first signs of resistance in our community.

At that time, my organization had been working day and night to muster support for a constitutional amendment to affirm our commitment to traditional marriage. The gay-rights agenda of the left was becoming a much bigger threat, and we knew something had to happen. Evangelical Christians were very active in Florida and Ohio during the campaign. One of the most effective teams traveled the entire state of Florida to talk about the importance of traditional marriage, and thousands of people of all races and persuasions responded to the message. They responded at the polls as well; by increasing the percentage of minority votes, our efforts gave a slight edge to the Republicans. It was just enough to give the GOP a surprising victory in the general election.

Statistics after the election showed that twice as many people in Ohio voted for the Republicans in that election than ever before. There was also a strong correlation between the number who voted for the president and the number who voted for the marriage amendment. The amendment we helped to draft drew them over, and the fact that the Republicans had established their credentials as the party of traditional moral values was enough to send George W. Bush back to the White House with conservative majorities in both houses of Congress.

We learned some important lessons during that campaign. The Democratic Party took the black community's votes and values for granted, and it cost them dearly.

While some politicians today are paying attention and listening to the African American community, many more continue to believe we're in lockstep with the Democrats and will never waver. Consequently, they don't take blacks seriously and they don't make any major policy decisions with our community's concerns in mind.

Well, I have news for those people. Things are changing. I have been deeply disappointed by the pro-abortion, pro-gay marriage, tax-and-spend policies of the Democrats for many years—and I'm not alone. More and more people are speaking out, standing up, and calling for a return to traditional norms and values. Today, the Democrats support issues that are increasingly controversial as they try to unravel the fabric of our way of life.

Same-sex marriage, unisex bathrooms and showers in schools, open borders, and unlimited immigration are all major concerns. And the Democrats are aggressively pushing a wide range of sexuality and gender-identity issues that defy common sense and ignore thousands of years of moral and cultural understanding. If we ignore these things, our families and our communities will suffer.

Democrats are aggressively pushing a wide range of sexuality and gender-identity issues that defy common sense and ignore thousands of years of moral and cultural understanding.

TAKING A CLOSER LOOK

The policies supported by the Democratic Party overwhelmingly reflect the values of their liberal base. But like more and more people in the black community, I am strongly pro-life, pro-family, and pro-traditional marriage. I oppose same-sex marriage, politically correct hate crimes laws, and the limitations on free speech advocated by Democrats. I also believe in fiscal restraint and limited government. On almost all of the issues that matter most to me, I identify more strongly with the Republican platform. So how can I give unwavering support to the Democratic Party when their worldview is precisely the opposite of my own?

My home base is in the Washington, DC, corridor, from which I have a clear view of the craziness that passes for government in this country. But all across the country, African Americans are beginning to question their relationship with the Democrats. Radical ideas coming from the far left have gone to such an extreme over the past decade that many die-hard Democrats feel as if they've been abandoned by their party. The only alternative, many are saying, is to reconsider our choices and take a closer look at the opposition.

If we expect to see real change in our neighborhoods, black voters are going to have to begin by looking a little closer at the Republican alternatives. For their part, the Republican Party will have to convince somewhere between 15 to 20 percent of black voters in this country that their long-term interests are better served by conservative Republican candidates who are supporting the issues that matter to blacks. It may be a hard sell—I don't have any misconceptions about that—but I am optimistic that in time and with constructive dialogue, it can happen.

There are a lot of people in our community who feel as I do about these things; consequently, there is a new dynamic in our midst, a new surge of African American political activism with strong conservative roots. This is a movement that is drawing its energy from the conservative moral values of what I've termed *the new black church.*

The message that's coming through loud and clear today is the understanding that moral choices make a difference. Social policies that undermine our moral choices ought to be avoided. Voting for a party because "we've always done it that way" is no longer acceptable. If we continue to give unwavering support to candidates who advocate radical left-wing social policies that no longer reflect our beliefs, we're only hurting ourselves. But if we align with those who agree with us on issues that truly matter, we'll be helping ourselves. Best of all, we will be taking a stand for righteousness and justice.

If we align with those who agree with us on issues that truly matter, we will be taking a stand for righteousness and justice.

As we include more minority interests in our national dialogue, we must add creative solutions for job creation and providing for the poor. We will need to be pro-life for both the unborn and for "the least of these" in our culture. (See Matthew 25:40.)

In the next chapter, we'll explore some new rules about safety as we journey on as a multiethnic, multicultural Christian family.

CHAPTER 9

BUCKLING EVERYONE'S SEAT BELT—HOLISTIC HUMANITY

There were some parts of our annual trip that seemed more dangerous than others. As we got older, we would try to relieve the boredom by sticking our hands and arms out of the windows—not a great idea on narrow roads! In some areas, we were warned to buckle our seat belts and stay in the car, especially if we were riding shotgun for a few miles.

I have spent the last ten years or so doing radio interviews with CNN, National Public Radio, and some of the local stations in my area. Since most of the programs were secular shows, someone would inevitably call in and say something along the lines of, "I don't think it's fair that the nation's laws reflect your values. I don't like your values. I don't want to live by your values!"

I didn't really know what to say the first time it happened. Over time, though, I was reminded that the U.S. government was created as a representative democracy. The founding fathers believed that the laws of our land should be based on the collective morality of its citizens. It didn't mean there was no room for Christianity, but rather that the views of the majority had to be considered. Those irate callers were actually saying they wanted their own individual brand of freedom and democracy rather than true democracy.

But if the laws of a representative democracy are supposed to reflect the collective values and morals of an entire nation, Christians should *not* keep silent in the culture.

I've already discussed the seven bridges of peace, including criminal justice reform, which brought me to the incredible story of Catherine Toney. The Christian community must teach our culture to make up the difference between righteousness and justice.

The Christian community must teach our culture to make up the difference between righteousness and justice.

HEALING THE RACIAL DIVIDE

Dr. Alveda King, the niece of Dr. Martin Luther King Jr., is another outspoken Trump supporter. Known as a conservative pro-life advocate, she has avoided political controversy. During a conversation with author Stephen Strang, she said she has a policy of not endorsing candidates but rather praying for God's will to be done. During the 2016 primaries, she backed Ben Carson who, like her, is a conservative, pro-life advocate. When Carson stepped down and endorsed Trump, she began working for the Trump campaign and was photographed with him on several occasions, sending a message to potential Trump supporters in the black community. [72]

The crucial issue for her was Trump's anti-abortion platform. She works with an organization called Priests for Life, a Catholic group headed by Father Frank Pavone. She hopes to get more blacks to reject the abortion option and stresses the *right to life* is the most fundamental civil right. Quoting her famous uncle, she says, "The Negro cannot win as long as he is willing to sacrifice the lives of his children for comfort and safety," adding, "How can the 'Dream' survive if we murder the children? Every aborted baby is like a slave in the womb of his or her mother. The mother decides his or her fate."

Tragically, Dr. King says, Planned Parenthood targets the black community for abortion. This is confirmed by research from the Life Issues Institute, which reports that nearly 80 percent of surgical abortion facilities are located within walking distance of black or Hispanic neighborhoods. [73]

In the United States, blacks make up approximately 13 percent of the population yet account for 36 percent of all abortions. Dr. King is constantly preaching this fact in the black community and has found a willing audience among African Americans who are Roman Catholic. She notes that Catholic support for Trump was 52 percent in 2016, compared to 42 percent for Hillary Clinton. In some key battleground states, she found that up to 18 percent of the black community voted for Trump.

Since his election, Donald Trump has extended his outreach to the black community in order to deal one-to-one with the problem of identity politics. The left has worked to divide this country for decades. In his book *Understanding Trump*, Newt Gingrich points out that the president has turned the tables on the Democrats by calling on all Americans "to celebrate their differences, but to never forget we are one people under God. ... At the bedrock of our politics will be a total allegiance to the United States of America, and through our loyalty to our country, we will rediscover our loyalty to each other." [74]

After his election, Trump knew he would be speaking to a fiercely divided electorate. So he offered a broader perspective, saying, "When you open your heart to patriotism, there is no room for prejudice. The Bible tells us, 'How good and pleasant it is when God's people live together in unity.' We must speak our minds openly, debate our disagreements honestly, but always pursue solidarity." This part of Trump's message was important because "it expresses an aspect of President Trump's personality that is completely overlooked by the media. To Trump," Gingrich writes, "bigotry cannot exist within a patriotic heart. To be racist—to hold any other American in low regard based on their gender, religion, race or heritage—is to be completely unpatriotic." [75]

Over the past two decades, I have been a frequent cable news contributor. Whenever given the chance, I have done my best to offer a message of mutual respect and reconciliation between the races. My message was much the same in September 2016 when I was invited by the National Religious Broadcasters to participate in a public debate with a former Bush administration staffer, a Never Trumper, who had taken the position of *anybody but Trump*.

As we began the second round of that debate, I took issue with many of my opponent's statements. My position was that Trump "may be the only one who's able to bring some substantive healing to the racial divide" and bring this country back together by advancing policies to improve education and economic opportunity for all Americans. Far too often, I pointed out, black and Hispanic voters have had to settle for the politics of grievance. But economic advancement for minority communities has been a priority of Trump's campaign—and he has continued to focus on all these things as president.

There's no denying that both parties have failed the people in these communities, but I believe this president is a change agent to move America forward by addressing the problems of race and class in substantive ways. And now, as I take the next step in this dialogue, dealing with what it would take to establish a real and lasting relationship between all Americans, I would like to address some thoughts on the importance of what I call "the Black Contract with America for Moral Values."

We want to see more pro-life justices on the Supreme Court and more honesty, understanding, and responsibility in law enforcement.

Education reform, economic development in urban areas, and family-oriented tax policies are every bit as important as prison reform, family formation, and religious liberty for our communities. We want to see more pro-life justices on the Supreme Court and more honesty, understanding, and responsibility in law enforcement. Trump's support for Israel—demonstrated dramatically by relocating the American embassy from Tel Aviv to Jerusalem—was important. These are all areas where Trump can make inroads with black voters, and we will all be well served by a commitment like that.

CHANGING THE OLD DYNAMIC

I suspect that the average person in the U.S. believes that the black community will always vote for Democratic candidates, primarily for their own personal economic interests. But this is a shallow generalization that takes into account neither the sophistication nor the growing spirituality of today's black voters. Men and women who make up the new black church are outspoken on issues such as same-sex marriage and abortion.

Every day and in practical ways, members of these churches are looking at contemporary society with a Bible in one hand and a laptop in the other. Our people have a history of looking to their Christian faith as a coping mechanism to help them deal with prejudice and adversity. But today, we understand that faith is essential in dealing with every aspect of life. Our faith is not a crutch: it's the standard by which we live, a statement of our core beliefs, and a guide to where we want our communities to be in the future.

Survey after survey shows that roughly half of all African American adults identify as born-again Christians. They are more likely than any other group to view their life as a gift from God, and they are the ethnic group most fervent to claim the promises of God for personal endurance and perseverance.

More blacks are beginning to think like their white evangelical Christian counterparts about politics.

We're not blind to the fact that the Democratic platform no longer reflects our views. It's no accident that more blacks are beginning to think like their white evangelical Christian counterparts about politics. And it's no accident that more people in the black community are coming to realize that many of the widely publicized liberal black spokespersons who populate most broadcast networks no longer speak for us. Many would say they're not the authentic voices of our people. Furthermore, they are no longer the only voices speaking up for black America. What's happening within black culture, the black church, and the black constituency is simultaneously happening within all minority communities. Rerouting is often painful, time-consuming, and intimidating.

Let me give you an example of forced rerouting: the coronavirus crisis has forced many minority churches to temporarily close, but their members still honor their clergy. They still expect their church leaders to help them integrate their faith with contemporary life. They want their lives and their votes to make a difference—and that means there will be many more changes to come. If we want to shake up the political apparatus, all we have to do is vote our conscience and make sure that our friends and family know what we're doing and why.

We don't have to convince everyone to follow our example. We only have to awaken a thinking core of Christian voters who understand the importance of voting for conservative moral issues. We don't need candidates to tell us what our values are. We already have our values. What we want to know is how we can make an impact on the political process.

CHAPTER 10

THE ROAD AHEAD: AVOIDING UNCLE TOM'S CABIN

As Eric and I became seasoned drivers, we took our turns behind the wheel. Relieving our parents got us to our destinations quicker than ever before. My brother was daring, but I was a little more conservative. Attending a wedding or a funeral became the easiest trips to manage, the purpose outweighing all else. On recreational trips or vacations, an up-to-date road map was crucial for our success. Time, destination, and even the route could vary. Of course, a GPS system would have simplified everything.

The question that this book attempts to answer is simply this: can our Christianity give us a road map to a better, more righteous, and more just America? The church in our nation needs a heart revolution, a spiritual awakening, and a renewed vision. We Christians are the only group who can practically unite our nation's zip codes and different ethnicities. True human dignity will only be discerned, developed, and celebrated in the context of the theological perspective that we all have been made in the image of God. We also must rediscover the inalienable rights and responsibilities cited in our Constitution.

In the first chapter of this book, we discussed the fact that our destinies are intertwined. In the second chapter, we concluded that we must select a common destination. In chapter eight, we laid out the proposition that a land filled with righteousness and justice is our unifying dream or desire.

As we think about *empowering* minorities and reaffirming the American dream, are we in danger of becoming de facto Uncle Toms?

Ironically, when abolitionist Harriet Beecher Stowe wrote her novel detailing the horrors of slavery, the hero was Uncle Tom himself.

I know the term must make you cringe, as it does me, but it didn't always have a negative connotation. Today, the term Uncle Tom has come to mean sellout or someone who has betrayed their race. Ironically, when abolitionist Harriet Beecher Stowe wrote the 1852 novel *Uncle Tom's Cabin*, detailing the horrors of slavery, the hero of the story was Uncle Tom himself. He was portrayed as a Christ-like figure who demonstrated more Christian virtues than his slave masters. History buffs may recall that *Uncle Tom's Cabin* helped to fuel the pre-Civil War antislavery movement. Even though Maine had few slaves, about 9,400 men from the state died fighting for the Union. All throughout New England, the image of Uncle Tom inspired white Christians to defend the human rights of slaves.

When Beecher Stowe did research for her book, she came across the story of a former Maryland-born slave named Josiah Henson who wrote an 1849 book about his life entitled *The Life of Josiah Henson, Formerly a Slave, Now an Inhabitant of Canada, as Narrated by Himself.*

Over time, Henson's faith-filled life was forgotten and nearly discredited. Until recently, I never knew that Henson had written a book about his life and had met personally with Beecher Stowe. He personally helped to free 119 other slaves and eventually met the Queen of England on March 5, 1877. And sixteen years after the end of the Civil War, President Rutherford B. Hayes received him at the White House.

An almost supernatural favor rested on *Uncle Tom's Cabin.* In an article for *Smithsonian Magazine*, Jared Brock wrote:

> Stowe wasn't concerned about the politics. To her, an ardent abolitionist and daughter of a world-famous preacher, slavery was a religious and emotional challenge. Her goal, as stated in the first edition preface, was "to awaken sympathy and feeling for the African race." On this point she certainly hit her mark, with many moderate antislavery advocates praising the book for putting a human face on slavery. If the Fugitive Slave Act of 1850 had been a tipping point, then *Uncle Tom's Cabin* was a hard shove toward abolitionism. [76]

In the past few decades, I have been called an Uncle Tom on many occasions. It was meant as a slur and a negative declaration of who I am. But those who embrace the road map that I have laid out in this book may also be misunderstood. We may be labeled and vilified. Whether you are a minority or a white person, reforming America's culture and returning this nation to its traditional roots will no doubt create some enemies. In the words of Grammy Award-winning Christian artist Kirk Franklin, "Do you want a revolution?" If so, there is a price to be paid.

POTHOLES ON THE ROAD TO FREEDOM

If you have visited our nation's capital in the last twenty years and driven more than fifteen minutes away from the Capitol, you have been delayed by road construction. It's almost as though we have declared a war on potholes. They are everywhere!

Our region's time and resources would not allow us to fix all the roads at once. Therefore, our beautiful city is doing constant upgrades. Even at the height of the coronavirus pandemic, aggressive work was done while traffic was at a low ebb. Mobilizing our collective resources and national courage to fight injustice in the U.S. is very similar to the District of Columbia's war on potholes. If we are to maintain the brilliance of our dreams and the consistency of our national philosophies, we must address the potholes on the road to freedom as each new generation begins to vote.

We must address the potholes on the road to freedom as each new generation begins to vote.

Although I want to celebrate how far we have come, we should also take a look at our past.

THE BROKEN MORAL COMPASS

In the early days of slavery in America, blacks were not allowed to congregate for religious purposes, nor were they permitted to preach or become ordained to ministry. The gospel was withheld from them.

For economic reasons, whites did not want blacks to be converted to Christianity because they believed only infidels or unbelievers could be enslaved. After paying thousands of dollars for their workforce, plantation owners did not want to give their slaves the message of the gospel. So throughout the Americas, education, citizenship, and economic opportunity were only given to those who converted to Christianity.

During the Great Awakening of the mid-eighteenth century, men like John Wesley, George Whitefield, and others began to preach that slavery should be abolished. This revival had a tremendous effect in the North as more people came to Christ. After dealing with Christ's claims for personal righteousness, they felt compelled to work for social justice. They believed that if they were going to really live for Christ, they had to treat others with Christian charity. Thousands of blacks in the South were saved during the Great Awakening, but their owners stopped short of embracing the full message of this revival.

Long before the outbreak of the Civil War, President Abraham Lincoln was deeply concerned about the problem of slavery. For many, the Civil War was a holy battle for social justice. Interestingly, Robert E. Lee, the head of the Southern army, was a valiant, courageous, and religious man who prayed and really feared God. Yet he led the Confederates who opposed justice for the slaves. Consequently, he did not receive God's blessing, his efforts were thwarted, and he lost the war.

In a real sense, the issue of slavery was God's lightning rod during that cataclysmic era. During the Reconstruction period, the Republican Party was filled with many blacks, yet America missed the opportunity to create a colorless society. At the turn of the twentieth century, God used the church as an ark to transport large numbers of blacks into an emerging new world of prosperity. Many moved from the South to the North as a part of the Industrial Revolution, but they took their churches with them. At least 70 percent of the black community in that era were members of a church. Thus, the local church had tremendous influence, and black pastors spoke out on political as well as spiritual issues.

Some may argue that we live in a post-racial society, especially since the United States has already elected its first African American president. How I wish it were true. There's work to be done and more territory to take.

A KINGDOM AGENDA

The African American church continues to be a mouthpiece for God, speaking truth to liberate all people both spiritually and in the natural realm. But our pulpits are no longer confined to a church building; God is using new voices such as Dr. Alveda King to unapologetically speak to the urgent issues confronting this country.

Unfortunately, the issue of identity politics that has become the Democrats' main appeal to black voters is a fact of life in most of America. While there are scores of black evangelicals and pro-family Catholics striving to restore balance and mutual respect between the races, the political left prefers to use groups like Black Lives Matter and Antifa to blast so-called *white privilege*. They use the compliant mainstream media to broadcast the conflict and sow dissension between the races.

The left uses a compliant mainstream media to broadcast conflict and sow dissension between the races.

My white conservative friends are offended by the phrase *white privilege*, which seems to suggest that whites have not worked for their positions or achievements in the context of our modern society. When used by minorities, the phrase is often an attempt to highlight injustice and the potholes on the minority journey to equal access and equal achievement.

Throughout American history, the Christian church has had seasons of brilliant action and seasons of disappointing weakness. Too often, it has done too little to combat the latter.

Our goal, in this work, was not to increase the level of acrimony and anger, either in the body of Christ or in the culture at large, but to call for a new level of understanding and cooperation to bring the nation back to God and create an atmosphere of brotherhood and shared values for all our people.

Naturally, we need government, business, law enforcement, and community stakeholders to partner with us. However, we believe the glue that will keep our communities and our nation together will always be the church and its dedicated faith leaders.

PRAYER WILL GET US THERE

Nothing was more exciting to Eric and me than when we would finally arrive at our destination on those road trips. Even if we had to endure a flat tire, inclement weather, long detours, and rough roads, we kept on driving. One thing is certain, however: without fuel in our gas tank, we could never have left our driveway.

I believe prayer is the fuel that ignites a revolution, whether you are a soccer mom wanting to take back your child's school from liberal bullies, a doctor who refuses to perform an abortion because it violates your Christian convictions, or someone facing retribution because you refuse to attend your gay boss's wedding. Nothing moves the heart of God to intervene in the affairs of human beings like prayer.

Nothing moves the heart of God to intervene in the affairs of human beings like prayer.

My weapon of choice in fighting for values of righteousness and justice is prayer. It's true that faith without works is dead (see James 2:26), but our prayers release our faith and concomitant steps of action take us toward our goals. The Lord's Prayer says, "Thy kingdom come, thy will be done on earth as it is in heaven." In order for us to accomplish God's will on earth, we must first seek His face.

I discovered in writing this book that the heart cry of the African slaves who came to this land in 1619 must have been "God free us and give our descendants safety and dignity in this strange land." The following year, white Puritans must have prayed a similar prayer for religious freedom. Therefore, they wrote the Mayflower Compact, which began:

> In the name of God, Amen. We, whose names are underwritten, the Loyal Subjects of our dread

Sovereign Lord King James, by the Grace of God, of Great Britain, France, and Ireland, King, defender of the Faith, etc.: Having undertaken, for the Glory of God, and advancements of the Christian faith, and the honor of our King and Country, a voyage to plant the first colony in the Northern parts of Virginia…

After their prayers, the Puritans and other colonists rolled up their sleeves and began to build a new society built upon their revelation of Christ and His word.

In April 2020, I was invited to go to the White House on Good Friday to give the Easter prayer. I was as ready as I was ever going to be because I had been praying for some time about what to say. To my astonishment, the words that I prayed in the Oval Office are also a reflection of our nation's founders and my heart's cry for the upcoming election. Here's an excerpt of what I prayed:

Thank you, Mr. President. First of all, let me say thank you for the job you're doing—you and the vice president—to protect our nation. … Good Friday, as we prepare to pray, is one of the darkest days in the Christian faith in that Christ stood in substitution for our sin. But the resurrection is our victory. But it parallels with the Passover. I'm going to read two verses and pray out of them about what we want to have happen. We want this plague to pass over. We want everyone in America to be safe. Psalm 105 says: "He brought them out with silver and gold, and there was none feeble among His tribes." Verse 39 goes on to say: "He spread a cloud for covering, and fire to give light in the night." Let us pray: Lord, let the death angel pass over. Let there be a mitigation of this plague, this disease. Let medical science come forth. Lord, let us come out with a thriving economy. That silver and gold spoken of in that passage, let it be our portion. And then, God, as we face other challenges in the future, Lord, cover us with a cloud by day and a fire by night. But in this great land that was set up to glorify your name, we want to break (the powers of darkness), we come against the spirit of division. Lord, let *E Pluribus Unum* be a reality in us. Let there be a uniting of America. Heal the divide between race, class, and gender. Once again, give this great man, our president, and give the vice president wisdom beyond their natural limitations. Give them insights so they can cover us, lead us, and bless us. We bless them and America in Jesus's name. Be encouraged. Hope is on the way. Amen.

THERE IS HOPE FOR AMERICA

During our travels, I don't think there was ever a time that my family was on our way somewhere and decided to turn around and go back home. No matter what, we kept driving. I have used this book to make the case for a better America, but there's much more to be done. I'm calling on minorities, especially African Americans, to move forward to a better future for our children's children. But there can be no going back to the broken promises of the Democratic Party.

THREE TOOLS FOR CONSERVATIVES

We have all been given a degree of influence to take more territory for conservative values, whether in our homes, churches, schools, or communities at large. And I believe there are three tools in particular that will help us maintain the White House on Election Day 2020.

1. *Pray strategically.* Some theologians call this identificational repentance and prayer for the generational destiny of their people. Daniel, Nehemiah, and Ezra prayed in this way, with amazing results.

2. *Preach a cultural gospel.* As the Babbie Mason song says, "Each one should reach one." Tell your family, friends, and all the people they know to spread the word to vote according to their Christian values. Just like modern-day evangelists, we must be ready to give an answer concerning the hope we have. (See 1 Peter 3:15.)

3. *Practice what you preach.* Register to vote and get others to do the same. We want to see a sea of souls at the polls come Election Day. Just 50 percent of Christian Americans are registered to vote, with only one-fourth of Bible-believing Christians actually following through and casting ballots.

This year, minorities must take a radical step and come off of the Democratic plantation. We must break the stranglehold that the Democratic Party has on our people, while enticing Republican strategists to reach just 8 or 10 percent more minority votes. This shift will take the kind of courage exhibited by biblical prophets. I repeat:

1. Pray

2. Preach

3. Practice

A new day is coming! A third great awakening is beginning. Re-read this book, buy one for your friends, and let's save our nation by bringing it back to its spiritual roots.

ABOUT THE AUTHOR

Harry R. Jackson Jr. is an American Christian preacher and Pentecostal bishop who serves as the senior pastor at Hope Christian Church in Beltsville, Maryland, and as the presiding bishop of the International Communion of Evangelical Churches. He is the founder and chairman of the High Impact Leadership Coalition, composed of ministers who actively promote socially conservative causes. Bishop Jackson is also a co-founder of the Reconciled Church Initiative, which seeks to bring racial healing to the church and America.

He has authored several books, including *You Were Born for More: Six Steps to Breaking Through to Your Destiny*, *The Way of the Warrior: How to Fulfill Life's Most Difficult Assignments*, and *In-Laws, Outlaws, and the Functional Family: A Real-World Guide to Resolving Today's Family Issues*. With George Barna, he co-authored *High Impact African American Churches*, which received the Silver Medallion award from the Evangelical Christian Publishers Association.

Bishop Jackson earned a B.A. in English from Williams College and an MBA from Harvard Business School. He has appeared as a guest on *The O'Reilly Factor, Cross Fire, Face the Nation, CBS Evening News, BET Evening News, 700 Club*, and several other programs. He has also been featured in the *New York Times, Los Angeles Times, Baltimore Sun*, the *Washington Post*, the *Philadelphia Inquirer*, and other media outlets.

Bishop Jackson has two adult daughters and makes his home in Maryland. Bishop Jackson may be contacted at www.harryjacksonministries.com.

ENDNOTES

CHAPTER ONE: SHARED DESTINY

1. William H. Frey, *Diversity Explosion: How New Racial Demographics Are Remaking America* (Washington, DC: Brookings Institution Press, 2018).
2. Jenna Wang, "Asian Americans Post Largest Gains In Homeownership," *Forbes*, May 31, 2018 (www.forbes.com /sites/jennawang/2018/05/31/ asian-americans-post-largest-gains-in-homeownership/#68d490c4a643).
3. Arthur C. Brooks, *Love Your Enemies: How Decent People Can Save America from the Culture of Contempt* (New York: Broadside Books, 2019).

CHAPTER TWO: SHARED DESTINATION—A TIME FOR CHANGE

4. Chuck Stone, "Black Political Power in the Carter Era," *The Black Scholar*, Vol. 8, No. 4, (January-February 1977).
5. Ibid.
6. Ibid.
7. Kiron K. Skinner, "Ronald Reagan and the African American," *National Review*, February 21, 2011 (www.nationalreview.com/2011/02/ronald-reagan-and-african-american-kiron-k-skinner).
8. Ibid.
9. Jonathan Easley, "Black leaders say African American support in presidential primary is fluid," The Hill, October 30, 2019 (thehill.com/homenews/campaign/468005-black-leaders-say-african-american-support-in-presidential-primary-is-fluid).
10. Yen Nee Lee, "2020 US presidential election is Trump's to lose, says BET founder Bob Johnson," CNBC, Nov. 29, 2019 (www.cnbc.com/2019/11/29/2020-election-is-trumps-to-lose-says-bet-founder-bob-johnson.html).
11. Matthew J. Belvedere, "BET founder Robert Johnson on Trump: 'I give the president credit for doing positive things,'" CNBC, Sept. 12, 2019 (www.cnbc.com/2019/09/12/robert-johnson-gives-trump-credit-for-doing-positive-things.html).
12. Jack Brewer, "Why African American Voters May Sit This One Out," FOXBusiness, Nov. 8, 2016 (www.foxbusiness.com/politics/why-african-american-voters-may-sit-this-one-out).
13. Ibid.
14. Jackie Danicki, "Dave Chappelle Defends Trump, Rips Clinton," *Observer*, Nov. 5, 2016 (observer.com/2016/11/dave-chappelle-defends-trump-rips-

clinton-shes-not-right-and-we-all-know-it).

15. P. R. Lockhart, "There is no single 'black vote.' There are many," *Vox*, Nov. 4, 2019 (www.vox.com/identities/2019/11/4/20926701/black-voters-democratic-primary-2020).

16. Ibid.

17. "Democratic National Committee: Resolution Regarding the Religiously Unaffiliated Demographic," Secular Coalition for America, August 26, 2019 (secular.org/wp-content/uploads/2019/08/DNC-Resolution-on-the-Nonreligious-Demographic.pdf).

18. Dave Andrusko, "More Black Babies in New York City are Killed in Abortions Than Born Alive," *LifeNews*, July 12, 2018 (www.lifenews.com/2018/07/12/more-black-babies-in-new-york-city-are-killed-in-abortions-than-born-alive).

19. Thomas B. Edsall, "No One Should Take Black Voters for Granted," *The New York Times*, Sept. 11, 2019 (www.nytimes.com/2019/09/11/opinion/black-voters-democrats-2020-election.html).

20. Ibid.

CHAPTER FOUR: FOLLOWING NEW DIRECTIONS; UNDERSTANDING NEW GOVERNMENT AND YOUNGER VOTERS

21. Rawn James Jr., *Root and Branch: Charles Hamilton Houston, Thurgood Marshall, and the Struggle to End Segregation* (New York, NY: Bloomsbury Press, 2010).

22. "Southern Poverty Law Center Linked to FRC Shooting in Chilling New Interrogation Video," Family Research Council, April 25, 2013 (www.frc.org/newsroom/southern-poverty-law-center-linked-to-frc-shooting-in-chilling-new-interrogation-video).

23. Ayesha Rascoe, "Trump Campaign Makes Pitch to Black Neighborhoods. Will It Connect?" NPR, March 8, 2020 (www.npr.org/2020/03/08/812996151/trump-campaign-makes-pitch-to-black-neighborhoods-will-it-connect).

24. David J. Harris Jr., Why I Couldn't Stay Silent: One Man's Battle as a Black Conservative (Redding, CA: NewType Publishing, 2018)

25. "Exit Polls," CNN Politics, updated Nov. 23, 2016 (www.cnn.com/election/2016/results/exit-polls/national/president).

26. Elizabeth Podrebarac Sciupac and Gregory A. Smith, "How religious groups voted in the midterm elections," Pew Research Center, Nov. 7, 2018 (www.pewresearch.org/fact-tank/2018/11/07/how-religious-groups-voted-in-the-midterm-elections).

27. "Evangelical Christians are racially diverse – and hold diverse views on immigration," The Conversation, Nov. 1, 2018 (theconversation.com/evangelical-christians-are-racially-diverse-and-hold-diverse-views-on-immigration-102329).

28. "Evangelical and Non-evangelical Voting & Views of Politics in America – Part 1," LifeWay Research (lifewayresearch.com/votingandpoliticalviews).

29. Elana Schor, "Trump's black voter outreach looks in part to the pews," *AP News*, Jan. 17, 2020 (apnews.com/47b6ce25616284d518f6a9cd04a06c43).

30. Doree Lewak, "Why these black New Yorkers are voting for Trump in 2020," *New York Post*, Feb. 29, 2020 (nypost.com/2020/02/29/why-these-black-new-yorkers-are-voting-for-trump-in-2020).

31. Rod Dreher, "Black Evangelical: 'White People, Chill Out,'" *The American Conservative*, Dec. 7, 2019 (www.theamericanconservative.com/dreher/black-evangelical-white-people-chill-out).

32. Ibid.

33. Janelle S. Wong, *Immigrants, Evangelicals, and Politics in an Era of Demographic Change* (New York: Russell Sage Foundation, 2018).

34. Janelle Wong, "Untapping the Potential of Black, Latino, and Asian American Evangelical Voters," *The American Prospect*, June 6, 2018 (prospect.org/culture/untapping-potential-black-latino-asian-american-evangelical-voters).

35. Janelle Wong, "Immigrants, Evangelicals, and Politics in an Era of Demographic Change," Russell Sage Foundation (www.russellsage.org/publications/immigrants-evangelicals-and-politics-era-demographic-change).

36. Jens Manuel Krogstad and Mark Hugo Lopez, "Black voter turnout fell in 2016, even as a record number of Americans cast ballots," Pew Research Center, May 12, 2017 (www.pewresearch.org/fact-tank/2017/05/12/black-voter-turnout-fell-in-2016-even-as-a-record-number-of-americans-cast-ballots).

37. Ibid.

38. Jordan Misra, "Voter Turnout Rates Among All Voting Age and Major Racial and Ethnic Groups Were Higher Than in 2014," Census Bureau, April 23, 2019 (www.census.gov/library/stories/2019/04/behind-2018-united-states-midterm-election-turnout.html).

39. CT Editors, "Why Latino Evangelicals Vote Beyond Immigration," *Christianity Today*, Nov. 7, 2018 (www.christianitytoday.com/ct/2018/november-web-only/latino-evangelicals-protestants-trump-voting.html).

40. Kori Schake, "The Republican Party Needs Millennials to Survive," *The Atlantic*, July 17, 2019 (www.theatlantic.com/ideas/archive/2019/07/gop-needs-millennial-voters/594034).

CHAPTER FIVE: TRAVELING TOGETHER TOWARD A NEW CONSENSUS

41. Harry R. Jackson Jr., *The Truth in Black and White* (Lake Mary, FL: Front Line Books, 2008).

42. *Glory*, directed by Edward Zwick (1989; TriStar Pictures).

43. Executive Order 10925—Establishing the President's Committee on Equal Employment Opportunity, March 06, 1961, The American Presidency Project (www.presidency.ucsb.edu/documents/executive-order-10925-establishing-the-presidents-committee-equal-employment-opportunity).

44. Louis Freedberg, "Fifty years after desegregation, wide racial and ethnic achievement gaps persist in Berkeley," *EdSource*, July 5, 2019 (edsource. org/2019/fifty-years-after-desegregation-wide-racial-and-ethnic-achievement-gaps-persist-in-berkeley/614645).

45. Stewart Lawrence, "Why Trump's Gains With Black Voters Could Swing The 2020 Election," *The Federalist*, Dec. 9, 2019 (thefederalist. com/2019/12/09/why-trumps-gains-with-black-voters-could-swing-the-2020-election).

46. Peter Baker, "Trump Reaches Out to Black Voters," *The New York Times*, Nov. 8, 2019 (www.nytimes.com/2019/11/08/us/politics/trump-black-voters. html).

47. Charles Bethea, "Donald Trump Makes an Awkward Pitch to Black Voters in Atlanta," *The New Yorker*, Nov. 10, 2019 (www.newyorker.com/news/dispatch/donald-trump-makes-an-awkward-pitch-to-black-voters-in-atlanta).

48. Vernon Robinson and Bruce Eberle, "The year the black vote switched: Will 2020 be 1936 in reverse?" *Washington Examiner*, Nov. 13, 2019 (www. washingtonexaminer.com/opinion/op-eds/the-year-the-black-vote-switched-will-2020-be-1936-in-reverse).

49. Ibid.

CHAPTER SIX: CROSSING THE DIVIDE: SEVEN BRIDGES TO PEACE

50. Harry R. Jackson Jr. and Tony Perkins, Personal Faith, Public Policy: The 7 *Urgent Issues that We, as People of Faith, Need to Come Together and Solve* (Lake Mary, FL: FrontLine, 2008).

51. Malcolm Gladwell, *The Tipping Point: How Little Things Can Make a Big Difference* (New York, NY: Back Bay Books, 2002).

CHAPTER SEVEN: PASSING THE HISPANIC AND ASIAN DRIVER'S TEST

52. CNN Editorial Research, "Hispanics in the US Fast Facts," *CNN* (www. cnn.com/2013/09/20/us/hispanics-in-the-u-s-/index.html).

53. CT Editors, "Why Latino Evangelicals Vote Beyond Immigration," *Christianity Today*, Nov. 7, 2018 (www.christianitytoday.com/ct/2018/november-web-only/latino-evangelicals-protestants-trump-voting.html).

54. National Hispanic Christian Leadership Conference News Release, "Growing Hispanic Population Signals Greater Pro-Life Support," NHCLC.org, (nhclc.org/growing-hispanic-population-signals-greater-pro-life-support).

55. Samuel Rodriguez and Robert C. Crosby, *When Faith Catches Fire: Embracing the Spiritual Passion of the Latino Reformation* (New York, NY: Crown Publishing Company, 2017).

56. Caleb Parke, "Hispanic pastors tour border facility lambasted by AOC and say they are 'shocked by misinformation,'" *Fox News*, July 2, 2019 (www. foxnews.com/politics/immigration-border-facility-aoc-hispanic).

57. Ibid.

58. Rodriguez and Crosby, *When Faith Catches Fire.*

59. Jack Jenkins, "In a close 2020 election, could a Hispanic evangelical swing vote be key?" *Religion News Service*, Oct. 28, 2019 (www.ncronline.org/news/politics/close-2020-election-could-hispanic-evangelical-swing-vote-be-key).

60. Abby Budiman, "Asian Americans are the fastest-growing racial or ethnic group in the U.S. electorate," Pew Research Center, May 7, 2020 (www.pewresearch.org/fact-tank/2020/05/07/asian-americans-are-the-fastest-growing-racial-or-ethnic-group-in-the-u-s-electorate).

61. Hansi Lo Wang, "Trump Lost More Of The Asian-American Vote Than The National Exit Polls Showed," *NPR*, April 18, 2017 (www.npr.org/2017/04/18/524371847/trump-lost-more-of-the-asian-american-vote-than-the-national-exit-polls-showed).

62. David Byler, "Politicians often overlook Asian American voters. They shouldn't, especially in 2020," *The Washington Post*, July 10, 2019 (www.washingtonpost.com/opinions/2019/07/10/politicians-often-overlook-asian-american-voters-they-shouldnt-especially).

63. Ibid.

64. Nicholas Wu, "Asian American leaders see growing political power going into 2020 election," *USA Today*, May 31, 2019 (www.usatoday.com/story/news/politics/elections/2019/05/31/asian-americans-vote-republicans-democrats-2020/1291441001).

65. Avik Roy and John Yoo, "The Republican Party Needs Asian Voters," *National Review*, March 7, 2019, (www.nationalreview.com/magazine/2019/03/25/the-republican-party-needs-asian-voters).

66. Steve Angeles, "Ron Falconi seeks to become the first Fil-Am in the Ohio state Senate," *Balitang America*, Oct. 10, 2019 (balitangamerica.tv/ron-falconi-seeks-to-become-first-fil-am-in-the-ohio-state-senate).

67. "Remarks by Vice President Pence at the White House Initiative on Asian Americans and Pacific Islanders Lunar New Year Celebration," WhiteHouse.gov, Jan. 27, 2020 (www.whitehouse.gov/briefings-statements/remarks-vice-president-pence-white-house-initiative-asian-americans-pacific-islanders-lunar-new-year-celebration).

CHAPTER EIGHT: THE DESTINATION: BIBLICAL JUSTICE AND RIGHTEOUSNESS

68. "Catherine Toney – 20 years – Immediate release per First Step Act," Can-Do Foundation (www.candoclemency.com/catherine-toney-20-years).

69. "An Overview of the First Step Act," Federal Bureau of Prisons (www.bop.gov/inmates/fsa/overview.jsp).

70. George Barna and Harry R. Jackson, *High Impact African American Churches: Leadership Concepts from Some of Today's Most Effective Churches* (Ventura, CA: Regal Books, 2004).

71. Jackson, *The Truth in Black and White*.

CHAPTER NINE: BUCKLING EVERYONE'S SEAT BELT—HOLISTIC HUMANITY

72. Stephen E. Strang, *God and Donald Trump* (Orlando, FL: Front Line Books, 2017).
73. Susan W. Enouen, "More Evidence Planned Parenthood Markets Abortion to Minorities," Life Issues Institute, June 14, 2016 (www.lifeissues.org/2016/06/pp-markets-abortion-minorities).
74. Newt Gingrich, *Understanding Trump* (New York, NY: Hachette Book Group, 2017).
75. Ibid.

CHAPTER TEN: THE ROAD AHEAD: AVOIDING UNCLE TOM'S CABIN

76. Jared Brock, "The Story of Josiah Henson, the Real Inspiration for 'Uncle Tom's Cabin,'" *Smithsonian Magazine*, May 16, 2018 (www.smithsonian-mag.com/history/story-josiah-henson-real-inspiration-uncle-toms-cabin-180969094).